D0926158

Walking Upright
on Foreign Soil
An Anthology

Summer Institute of Linguistics
Waxhaw, North Carolina

©1995 by Summer Institute of Linguistics
All rights reserved.
Printed in the United States of America
ISBN #1-878606-16-6

Acknowledgments

Walking Upright on Foreign Soil is an anthology of first-person experiences which illustrate maintaining or losing favor with host governments abroad. The editors are indebted to all who contributed to the collection. Each is identified in the context of his own account.

Thelma Johnston served as chief editor of this collection, choosing and composing stories from both written sources and interviews. Inspiration, direction, and content editing were provided by Dr. Richard Pittman. Joyce Gullman assisted with editing and proofreading. Nancy Navratil and Joyce Gullman keyboarded the text. Brian Tenny produced the camera-ready copy for the printer.

Table of Contents

Preface

Richard Pittman

This is a book for people who expect to be involved in projects overseas. It tells an expatriate what he does not want to hear: how to relate in a country not his own, to a persona who outranks him, who may strongly disagree with him, and whose culture, rather than that of the visitor, is the one to follow.

How-to books are a dime a dozen. But how-to books which suggest solutions to relations in which the other fellow makes the rules...?

This is only one such book, but it is one whose credibility is substantial. How can that be proven? By the means most often recommended as science: experimental application of the same principles, in the same manner, with the same alignment of heart and hands as described in the accounts contained herein.

x /

I

FIRST CONCERN: THEIR GOVERNMENT

If you call on, report and defer to, befriend, and involve host government officials in your work, you have paved the way to a cooperative atmosphere for your project.

———————

———————

Cameron Townsend:

We can do so much more, arm in arm with the (host) government. The government in turn gets so much more done for its people in linguistic matters by cooperating with us.

———————

Do we identify ourselves with them? Do we listen to their problems? To their headaches? To their ambitions? Do we study their needs with them? Do we ask their help? Do we consult them on matters of mutual concern? Do we invite them to our homes? Do we attend social affairs with them?

———————

I cannot recall that we have ever been rejected when we have followed the approach of identification, of submission, of respect, of mutual concern, of study, of reporting to our hosts.

A.

Recognize authority.

O King, Live Forever

Richard Pittman

"The powers that be are ordained by God." How can that be? It is preposterous! "How," some ask, "can Hindu, Muslim, Buddhist, Communist or atheist powers be ordained by God?"

Does Paul's statement mean that God ordained both the Pharaoh who knew Joseph and the Pharaoh who knew him not? It means just that. The first was ordained by God to save the lives of God's people through Joseph. The second was ordained by God as one upon whom God's power would be shown as a testimony to God's name throughout the whole earth. (Exodus 9:16; Romans 9:17)

Kay and I were married in 1936 and spent our first year together in El Paso, Texas, on the Mexico border. We had never heard of Cameron Townsend. And all we knew about Mexico was what we read in the El Paso papers. That was not flattering, to put it mildly. In fact, because all churches had been closed, the newspapers were printing very alarming stories, painting Mexico as being second only to the USSR in its far-left position. It is probably just as well that we did not know Townsend in those days. He was defending President Cardenas, and nearly all that the American papers said about Cardenas was bad. His excellent qualities were not yet clear at all to most Americans. But Townsend had met him and was deeply impressed. Never one to shy from the fray, he wrote a book, *The Truth about Mexico's Oil*, in Cardenas' defense when nearly every other American writer was attacking him.

In the summer of 1940 we met the Townsends, and by the late fall of that year we settled in Tetelcingo, where we saw quite a bit of them. Some time after our arrival I asked Mr. Townsend if it might be wise to try to meet a certain influential man (whom I named) in the hope that he would help us. "We do not 'try' to meet influential people," he replied. "But when God brings them our way and/or gives providential encounters with them, we try to be faithful friends."

I could see this in practice, as he sought to be a faithful friend to Cardenas. Nor was it a one-way street. He was not "using" Cardenas for what he could get out of him; he was seeking to give help also.

In 1976 I had the privilege of attending a dinner at which former President Cardenas' widow was installed as president of the patronato which sponsors SIL in Mexico. As I witnessed the strong affection, not only between the Townsends and Mrs. Cardenas, but also between them and innumerable other intimate Mexican friends, I could see the sweet fruit of forty years being borne. It was moving indeed.

Nor was it an empty gesture. It came at a time when our work worldwide had been under attack as never before. In at least four of the countries where we work there had been close-down threats or orders—all within the space of a few months.

But isn't it a misuse of an administrator's time to be doing things for a possibly misguided head of state rather than for the members of the organization to which he belongs? Daniel no doubt did a great deal for Shadrach, Meshach, and Abednego. But he surely gave his first attention to King Nebuchadnezzar and to the king's successors. In fact, his devotion to them was so deep and firm that when King Darius, who had thrown him to the lions, asked if his God had been able to deliver him, Daniel's immediate words were, "O King, live forever!" Was he honest? Should he not, if he were truthful, have replied, "I am safe, Mr. King, but no thanks to you"?

The salvation from famine which Joseph was able to provide for his father and brothers was not achieved by giving them his undivided attention. It came as a result of his loyal service to the Gentile king of Egypt.

Jesus Himself, when asked if it was right to pay taxes to the foreign emperor who was governing the Jewish people, said, "Render to all their dues: tribute to whom tribute is due; custom to whom custom; fear to whom fear; honour to whom honour." (Romans 13:7) There are many Christians who would like to do Bible translation in countries which are not their own without rendering to the government authorities of those countries the recognition which is their due. No way. Or, as they say in Papua New Guinea, "No got!"

The Peacock Block

Jim Dean, Bill Oates, and I were surveying the languages of Papua New Guinea in order to determine whether SIL should seek to work there. On our way we met a district officer who recommended we consider establishing headquarters on a piece of property known as the "Peacock Block" because a man by that name had once planned to grow coffee there. It seemed so ideal that we replied to the district officer that we would like to lease it. Would he help us? He would and did.

But he was a Catholic and we were Protestants. That made no difference to him. He rolled up his sleeves and did what we needed in a serious, professional way. Too many persons, however, fancy that the main hope of being allowed to do Bible translation in a given country lies with the Protestant officials in the country. It is not so. Not only the "powers that be" but also their ranks in their hierarchy are ordained by God. And a part of what God has ordained in our day is that, in relations with expatriates, at least, the State is over the Church. It is a serious mistake, therefore, for expatriates to seek to circumvent established protocol in host countries by looking to nationals of their own political or religious persuasion to run interference for them.

Peter's opinion

A man so blunt and forthright as Peter might have been expected to speak his mind in no uncertain terms to the Roman officials who crucified his Lord and gave Peter himself a hard time. Let's ask him. "Peter, what is your opinion on this touchy subject of what our attitude should be to government authorities?"

"For the sake of the Lord submit yourselves to every human authority: to the emperor, who is the supreme authority, and to governors (e.g., Pontius Pilate!) who have been appointed by him to punish evildoers and to praise those who do good. For God wants you to silence the ignorant talk of foolish people by the good things you do...respect everyone, love your fellow believers, have reverence for God, respect the emperor." (I Peter 2:13-17)

The Consolations of Government Work

Richard Pittman

I doubt that there is anyone who has been more troubled by assignment to government work than I was. I enjoyed linguistics and translation work greatly. Village living was very much my bag of tea (as Myra Lou Barnard says); city living is like purgatory to me.

To describe my worst experience at government work I must change the names of the people and places involved because the "villain" is still at large.

So I shall call the place "Babylon" and my tormentor "Rabshakeh" ("Rab" for short). The torment he was putting me through consisted of wrapping me cunningly in red tape. Our visas were being held up; he was almost certainly the cause. But every attempt I made to discover the problem resulted only in a fresh runaround—more shadowboxing and wheel-spinning. This could have been borne if I had had even so much as evenings with my family. But the circumstances were such that I did not even have Kay with me. Days stretched into weeks, and six weeks went by with no perceptible progress.

One day I was again making the fruitless round of government offices and again having to cool my heels waiting for some minor official to show up. As I waited my eyes wandered to a chart of names and rank of officials in the Babylonian Ministry of Education. There was Rabshakeh's name, mocking me. And his high rank seemed very secure. But as my little-hope eyes wandered higher, they were suddenly riveted by another name: Cyrus. Cyrus! I thought. I know him! He is first rate. And he is over Rab! I rubbed my eyes. There must be some mistake. But no! The chart was still there, and Cyrus was still listed as outranking Rabbie. I made a mental note to try to see him.

It did not work out immediately, but a few days later I found myself, at the end of a long day's fruitless work, in the building which housed his office. Wearily I started up the stairs to see what I could do. As I went up the narrow flight, I had to make way for a man coming down. Our eyes met. He stopped uncertainly. "Don't I know you?" he queried.

"Yes, sir," I replied. "I am Richard Pittman of the Summer Institute of Linguistics. I am on my way to seek an appointment with you."

"I cannot see you today," said Cyrus (for that is who it was), "but check with my secretary. I will be glad to see you next week."

The session with Cyrus the following week was better than I had dared to hope. In fact, after listening carefully to our problem, he asked if I could come to lunch with him and a few other officials a week or so later. I said I would be delighted.

The morning of the luncheon dawned bright and clear—auspicious in every way except that I had a bad sore throat. I arrived at the place appointed (Cyrus' office) and discovered to my delight that three other old friends had been invited: Melzar, Arioch, and Hegai. My throat condition by that time had become a laryngitis so bad that I could hardly talk. No one seemed to notice, however; each of them had a good deal to say. Most voluble was Rabbie, who had no doubt been invited in order to hear the message that the other four were supporting me.

There was no immediate change following the luncheon. A few months later, however, to my astonishment and delight, I learned that Rabbie had been transferred right out of the department. The new structure which replaced him was one with which we could work much better. Visas began to come through. From a dismal, no-headway round of calls in Babylon, the government relations job became one where progress could be seen and fruit savored.

Avoiding the Crunch

Steven Sheldon

When the crunch came in Brazil, we did not have influential friends who could help. Our academic public relations were very good, and we had good relationships with the Indian Agency. This was obviously not enough, and, as Darcy Ribeiro, the man responsible for our invitation to come to Brazil, said to me, "Steve, you must realize that unfortunately we academic types do not have much political clout in this country. You must seek to build friendships with military and ministerial level people." He added that he felt close ties with the Catholics were absolutely essential.

For many years we as a branch said that we could not afford to place emphasis on government relations. Only one man had been assigned to do this type of work, and his was a half-time-or-less project. This was not the fault of previous administrations but rather the fault of "we the people." Whenever attempts were made to beef up the government relations area, a loud cry went up from teams: "Don't bother us!" I know because I was one of those saying it! We kept teams in the language groups with this approach, but when government problems and attacks came, we did not have government or military friends who knew us well enough to help.

Fortunately God gave us some key contacts and we were spared being expelled from Brazil. Unfortunately it still took me, and I believe others as well, a long time to come to the point of seeing how wrong we had been to try to work without making and maintaining friendships with military, government, and Catholic people.

Ethel Wallis summed this up in the April 1979 *Intercom*: "In investigating the reasons for serious problems in some countries, I have discovered that original SIL principles and practice were not followed. To allay suspicions and build bridges for subsequent academic and spiritual activity, strong overt links with host governments must be established and maintained."

To the Palace on a Scooter
in the Rain

John Kyle

Les Troyer, director of the Philippine branch, had been in Manila looking for property on which to build our headquarters. He ran out of time and turned his calls over to me. He had called in the office of the executive secretary, who was the top administrator for the president. SIL had not yet made contact with him. Left at his office was a copy of the fine book by Huxley about SIL's work in Latin America.

I made an appointment and arrived at the presidential palace on my scooter on a rainy afternoon, wearing a fine barong tagalog shirt and a raincoat. This was my first call at the palace; I would not recommend making such a call alone, but no one else of our staff was in Manila at the time.

I was taken directly to the secretary's office where there were about one hundred people seeking help, each accompanied by a congressman or other influential government worker. Each audience was held openly for all to hear. The room was huge, with beautiful mahogany walls and floors, and a full staff on hand to assist the secretary, who was sitting behind a great desk.

Finally my time came and I was escorted to a chair in front of the desk. The secretary greeted me in a friendly manner. He had seen me sitting all alone out there and, having studied at Harvard, must have sensed how awkward I felt. He immediately invited me to sit in a vacant chair near him behind his desk and asked what he could do for me. I told him of our SIL work with the Department of Education among the language groups in his nation, explaining how we reduced unwritten languages to a written form and conducted literacy work among cultural minorities. He was most interested and asked a few questions.

I told him that since we had contracts with the Department of Education and the University of the Philippines, cooperating with the Philippine Air Force and the Signal Corps of the army, we wanted to request his assistance in locating some government land which could be leased to SIL for our headquarters in Manila. He made one phone call and spoke at some length to someone who I assumed was Secretary of Education Carlos Romulo. After talking for a while he began to direct his staff to make phone calls to such people as the Secretary of Agriculture to discuss certain parcels of land that he knew about. He issued commands in machine gun order and then brought an attorney to my side, assigning him to be my contact to follow up on the project.

Leaving the office, I ran out into a pouring rainstorm and over to the covered porch of the press office where many others were waiting out the storm. One of them said, "You are Mr. John Kyle, aren't you?" He introduced himself as the secretary's press officer and proceeded to tell me I had had a good audience with the secretary and that his boss was impressed with SIL and liked me. He told me that when Les Troyer brought the *Farewell to Eden* book about SIL's work in Latin America, he had reviewed it and advised the secretary to welcome the SIL representative because the group was doing some wonderful things for the minorities.

That day began a long and rewarding friendship with these men. The press secretary was later transferred to the office of the Secretary of Defense, where he was very helpful to SIL. We did eventually get a fine piece of land.

Homage to an Official
on His Birthday

Robert Schneider

A local Lima newspaper publicized a birthday reception honoring an outstanding Peruvian political leader. Friends were invited to attend the reception, and tickets could be purchased during the day at the hotel hosting the event. This is common practice in Latin America.

Jim Wroughton and I were quick to respond. We would help celebrate the birthday of a friend and at the same time recognize his position of authority. Many of the nation's leaders would be present. What a wonderful opportunity to greet acquaintances away from the telephones and other interruptions normal during a regular office interview with these same people!

During the reception Jim and I were able to speak with the Minister of Foreign Affairs (and to invite him to attend the graduation ceremonies of the bilingual teachers' training course at Yarinacocha), the Minister of Energy (who remembered with fondness his visit to our jungle center), and our boss, the Minister of Education. The president himself joined the group of orators extolling the guest.

As Jim and I looked around, we could see no other American (and few, if any, other foreigners). Yet, as we introduced ourselves as members of SIL, we were appreciatively recognized.

The Rewards of Reports

Carolyn Miller

Doing a survey of languages related to Bru was only part of the project. The survey completed, we Millers took time to return to government officials at the province, district, and village levels with letters of appreciation and samples of work done in the languages spoken in places under their jurisdiction.

"Two of the professors at Mahidol translated the sociolinguistic survey report into Thai, and we took it to district and village officials. We also took copies of phrase books and thesauruses that had been done by people from their area. I think this was a way of gaining prestige, not only for the authors but also for their languages," wrote Carolyn.

"I think they were surprised that we came back, but most seemed pleased. One of them said, 'Researchers come here and do their work, but we never learn any of the results.'"

A Little Bit of Sugar
Helps the Medicine Go Down

Richard Pittman

Sentimental gifts, while having little financial value, show appreciation for the person to whom they are given and recognition of his status. When the McKaughans and Pittmans first went to the Philippines, for example, we were all poor as church mice. Nothing but a direct revelation from God could show us what sort of gift was suitable for Ramon Magsaysay and his wife at that time.

But the Lord gave the revelation! Kay and Bobie McKaughan had put together a delicious combination of papaya and pineapple into a jam which we promptly christened "papinya." The next time we called at the Magsaysay residence, the husband was not home but his wife met us. We had nothing to offer but a small jar of papinya jam. But it was the perfect Proverbs 17:8 gift—"A gift is as a precious stone in the eyes of him that hath it..." It did not make them feel indebted to us but did give them a warm feeling for us.

The Moon and Dr. Morote

Allan Shannon

News reached us that the first U.S. space capsule had landed on the moon. Barb and I had been working with the Quechuas in Ayacucho, a small town high in the Andes Mountains of Peru. That night, as I walked outside under the beautiful starry sky, high on a mountaintop overlooking Ayacucho, I tried to picture a man walking on the bright lunar surface above me. My vision was then distracted by the headlights of a vehicle winding up the rocky mountain road from the city below. Who could be driving up here at this hour of night? I wondered.

As the vehicle approached the house, I saw that it was Dr. Efrain Morote Best and his wife. Dr. Morote was an old friend of Uncle Cam who had known of our work in Peru for years. At that time he was rector of the University of Huamanga in Ayacucho. He and his wife gave both of us an *abrazo* (embrace) and said, "Congratulations!" Barb and I were glad to see them, but I guess our faces showed bewilderment. "Surely you have heard," said Dr. Morote, "that the U.S. has just landed a man on the moon. We have come to congratulate you and your country for this historic event!"

I was taken aback by this remark since I knew that Dr. Morote was not particularly in agreement with U.S. politics and policies in Latin America. Seeing my surprised expression he said, "Don't you know that this is an historic milestone in U.S. progress in space? On behalf of the scientific world and especially Peru, we want to congratulate you North Americans for a job well done!"

We stammered our thanks and invited them in for a cup of coffee. They began then to reminisce about their days living at our Yarinacocha center when Dr. Morote was director of the bilingual education program for Indian schoolteachers. Even though I had known Dr. Morote for years and had heard many stories of how he had helped the indigenous peoples of Peru, I gained a new appreciation of this man. No matter what his political leanings were, Dr. Morote still recognized and appreciated the scientific efforts and advances of the United States because he had had the privilege of living and working with a great North American statesman, William Cameron Townsend.

The First Glue

Richard Pittman

Priorities and protocol

I was making instant coffee. It was back in the early days of powdered milk and nonfreeze-dried powdered coffee. And the old-time powdered milk was anything but "instant."

I popped a spoonful of powdered coffee into the cup and a spoonful of powdered milk. Then I poured in the hot water. I proceeded to stir—with diligence and patience. But all I got was a great clot of dumpling-like milk which steadfastly refused to dissolve. "Rats!" I exclaimed in disgust.

"Darling, you've got to put the milk in last," Kay soothed.

"What difference does it make?" I sulked.

"This difference," she explained, pointing to her own creamy-looking cup and my lumpy soup. "Put the milk in first and you get yours; put it in last and you get mine."

It was an important lesson in protocol. Or in ordered rules, if you dislike the word *protocol.*

There is a priority order for a foreigner calling on officials in a country whose friendship he hopes to gain. A high official does not appreciate learning from the grapevine that a visitor has arrived and is seeing those under him before seeking to see him.

But high officials are hard to see. How can a person waste time waiting to see the top man when those of lower rank are willing to see him without delay? By making his requests for appointments with the highest men as early as possible. If a man knows his office has been approached first, he can forgive the foreigner for seeing others while waiting for the appointment at the top. And remember that civil officials outrank religious.

Start at the top.

Isn't the danger of getting a negative reply greater if you start at the highest ranks first? No! Contrary to popular belief, the top man in a hierarchy is not the toughest man. He cannot afford to be.

In fact, he is obligated to be more lenient than those under him because he is the court of last resort. Also, he must strive in any type of government to get maximum credit for achievements, so must be the one saying most of the yeses. And in a really strict, totalitarian system he is the only one who can say yes. The lower echelon officials are expected to say no, wait, maybe, or I'll ask the boss.

Do not ask for an appointment with a really high official unless you are prepared to wait.

By "really high" we mean a president, cabinet officer, or ambassador. It is an insult to such a person to ask for an audience and then tell him you cannot accept the date, several days or a couple of weeks later. If he offers a date, you had better "break your neck" (meaning break some sacrosanct other plans) to take it. And having accepted, do not postpone or miss it for anything.

In relations with foreign organizations in-country, the State is over the Church.

It makes no difference whether it is a united "State-Church" society, an American style "no establishment of religion" society, or a Communist/atheist government. In all cases it is the national government, not a local religious group, which has the last word on whether visas will be issued to representatives of foreign groups.

But you know of groups which got in without approval of the national government? No doubt you do! But it is not the best way. Bypassing the national government is a precarious route for a foreign organization to follow, no matter how warm a reception it may experience from a nongovernment entity in the country for which entry permission is sought.

It is not the responsibility of a foreigner to decide, in a country not his own, which political group is good and which is bad.

God has repeatedly shown in amazing ways that He can and will use those in power to accomplish His purposes, regardless of the seeming impossibility of any situation. The suffering which Israel endured in Egypt became a powerful deterrent to Satan's attempts to drag them back there. The suffering which they endured in Babylon cured them from the grosser forms of idolatry. Cardenas, who was often called "Communist" by American newspapers, gave much personal support to Bible translation in his country.

Do not fancy that the main hope of being allowed to translate in a country lies with the Protestant officials of that country.

Not only the "powers that be" are ordained by God, but also the rank which they hold in the hierarchy. Strict recognition of and adherence to this order must be observed by a foreigner seeking permission for his organization to work in a given country. The temptation to bypass a higher official because he is a Muslim or Catholic or Communist must be resisted at all costs. God has used officials of every imaginable persuasion, functioning in their proper offices, to help His work forward in the way He wants it to go. A Catholic official, for example, in Papua New Guinea was extremely helpful to the PNG branch in arrangements for leasing the Ukarumpa property there.

Do not allow members of any SIL unit to make political pronouncements about countries which are not their own.

There is an almost overwhelming tendency, among persons raised in countries where freedom of speech is standard, to exercise the same freedom in countries where they are guests. Even if those are also "free speech" countries, the foreigner does not have the right to speak against conditions which he dislikes in such lands.

Do not allow yourself or any member of your organization to give propaganda material to nationals which they can use against friendly officials.

Dr. R. was dismissed as director of the National School of Anthropology in Mexico for allowing SIL to print gospel hymns and a few Scripture verses on the school press. In Mexico any such religious activity in a government school is strictly forbidden.

In the foolish years of my student days I kept getting tied in knots by the fanciful dilemmas teachers and other students posed because they made no mention of ordered rules or the ranking of laws.

"When a stoplight is red but a policeman is standing there waving you to go ahead, which do you do?" It is not a dilemma, because the policeman outranks the stoplight.

"Is it lawful for us Jews to pay taxes to the unlawful Roman emperor who imposes them?"

"Render to Caesar that which is Caesar's, and to God that which is God's."

Freedom is very precious. I am more thankful than I can say for the freedoms we enjoy. But when I drive up to a yield sign, I am not free to pull out in front of an approaching car which is not blocked by such a sign. Or, to put it another way, I am free to pour sand into the gas tank instead of gas, but if I do so I will not be free to drive that car very far.

How long should the priority of government relations continue?

I am a teacher of linguistics. And I enjoy teaching linguistics much more than I enjoy doing government relations work. I especially enjoy teaching linguistics to Christians. The enthusiastic response and the warm appreciation make it abundantly worthwhile. The response I get in some government offices, however, is cold, indifferent, unfeeling. No wonder I tend to drift into the teaching of linguistics and out of government relations work!

A similar development took place in one country. Our first contact with a certain government post was very friendly because we greatly needed their help and we knew it. We were therefore very deferential.

As God prospered the work our need for their help became less; but a succession of fine Christian people at the post proved easy and delightful to relate to, so relations continued to be excellent.

Then the Christians who loved to help us at the government post left, and a more matter-of-fact officer was appointed. We related to him in a formal way but little more. His help was not much needed and ours was not much offered, so relations cooled.

Then a dunning letter from an SIL department to which a government officer owed money provided a spark which ignited an explosion.

"You SIL people," the officer said, in effect, "love to receive favors but you are not so keen to give them." There followed a long list of good turns the government had done for SIL. "Furthermore," the officer continued, "you like to relate to and do things for those of your same religious persuasion, but you are slow to help those who differ with you."

Oh, that hurt! Townsend, from the day SIL was founded, had insisted that we must be good neighbors without regard to the religious views of those involved.

But almost certainly the most important point was left unspoken. The people at the post represented the host government. We found it easier and more enjoyable to relate to Christians than to government. The result was understandable: much thought and effort went into Christian relations; much less went into government relations. The priorities which had characterized the beginnings were gradually reversed.

It is not a better way. Government relations must have priority over religious relations not only at the start of a work but also continuously—right up to the end. And the order must be followed not only at the highest levels but also at the lowest. The first man to call on in even the humblest village is the headman, not the pastor. When this is done, both will be content. When it is not done, uneasiness and possible trouble will result.

But God won in the end. The wife of a man from the government post had a baby born at the SIL clinic. The unfeigned love and all-out help of the SIL doctor and nurses made amends for all.

"Man can do anything!" chortled an American official after a successful space mission. He failed to mention that, in order for the astronauts to return safely to earth, they had to reenter earth's atmosphere with their spaceship in exactly the right attitude, hitting their space-time "window" at exactly the right velocity on the right trajectory. Only as they submitted to the protocol of the laws of physics which governed their space flight could they safely complete it. And it is only as Christians submit to the protocol of the laws of human relations that they can successfully "do anything."

B.

Involve nationals.

Stranger in the Hangar
at Quitting Time

Richard Pittman

Everyone is glad when quitting time comes. The last man out of the hangar is happiest of all. He can close down, lock up, and head for home, supper, family, maybe a swim in the lake.

It was disconcerting, therefore, at the end of a hot day at the hangar to see a stranger wander in just at quitting time. Entertaining strangers is not a mechanic's job. But when a mechanic is the last man out, he has only two choices—either to brush rudely past such a visiting stranger or to courteously introduce himself and seek to be helpful.

Though grace for such a dilemma may seem to be in short supply when one is frazzled at the end of a long, hard day, the mechanic managed to summon up enough of it to greet the stranger and strike up a conversation. The visitor was inquisitive and asked more questions than a tired mechanic wanted to answer. But grace was sufficient to enable the mechanic to remain courteous until he could finally turn the visitor over to a person responsible for receiving such people.

Just before they parted the visitor pulled out a calling card and handed it to the mechanic, saying, "If I can ever be of help to you in Lima, look me up."

The JAARS man tucked the card into his pocket and forgot it. No one takes those polite gestures seriously...

No one, that is, until furlough rolls around and the immigration officials suddenly declare that the teenage son will not be allowed to leave the country in which he was born until he has put in his two years of compulsory military service. At that time young men were subject to the draft in America too, so the son was in double jeopardy. What to do?

Suddenly the forgotten calling card was remembered. Its giver was a colonel. Could he help?

"Not easy," mused the colonel, as they asked what he could do. "But I will try."

He tried and succeeded. The son was allowed to leave the country with his parents. Guess who remembered with thankfulness a hot, late-afternoon encounter when he had almost snubbed a visitor who had wandered in unannounced!

What Is the Occasion?

Richard Pittman

Ron and Ruth Gluck had family members home for the holidays. They were also looking for a way to honor and relate to the ambassador of Cameroon where they had served for many years. Might there be a way to put both circumstances together into one celebration?

Ah...there was! The first anniversary of the wedding of Robin and David Witmer was coming up. It could provide the ideal "excuse," the kernel on which nucleation could take place, the charged particle on which the snowflake could crystallize.

Would the ambassador and his wife be willing to come for such an observance? They were and they did! Ron described the event:

"Guests for the evening included Ambassador and Mrs. Pondi and their son Emmanuel, home from Cambridge for the holidays. Other guests were the Witmers and David, Ruth, and Neil Cummings visiting from Dallas.

Discussion centered on Emmanuel's studies in his pursuit of a graduate degree in international relations, activities of the Pondis' other son in Cameroon in banking, and a hilarious recounting (in French) of Cheryl Gluck's experiences in Cameroon.

"The Pondis obviously enjoyed these stories as they were in French and may have been the first noncritical feedback they have ever heard from a white person on experiences in Cameroon.

"Following the discussion, we sang several Christmas carols in English. Next, Mr. and Mrs. Pondi entertained us with several carols in Bassa. David Cummings then prayed, offering thanks to the Lord for our evening together and for God's blessing on our activities. Emmanuel, our son Charles, and our daughter Cheryl then wakened a guitar, drums, and piano for some lighter music, much to the delight of Mr. and Mrs. Pondi.

"It was a very positive evening and one which I believe will help cement our friendship with the Pondis. They brought a gift to Witmers."

Some of us, because of other duties, other priorities, or even lack of imagination, fail to recognize ideal opportunities to involve officials of host countries in celebration events. It may help to list some circumstances which are worth a celebration and hence give opportunity for additional contacts with officials: weddings, birthdays, anniversaries, visits of SIL members, graduations, receptions, farewells, reunions, dedications.

It is especially important to remember that a celebration honoring some citizen of the host country is more significant than one honoring an expatriate, and one which manages to honor both nationals and expatriates is best of all.

If you cannot think of an appropriate occasion to celebrate, make one!

Oh, by the Way
Al Wheeler

The visa situation was not very good in one of the countries where we worked. Because of criticism against us and pressures on the government, our official visa privileges were taken away and we were given six-month temporary visas. In certain cases the expiration date indicated that they could not be renewed. No one ever had to leave the country because his visa was denied; the Lord worked in every case to keep the people in the country. However, each had to make a trip in person every six months into a population center in order to process the necessary paperwork. This had not been necessary before and was quite a drain on translators' time.

Our administrators used various approaches to the government to explain our situation and the work of SIL. They asked the Foreign Relations Department about the possibilities of getting longer visas. The requests were received courteously, but for three years the same six-month visas were continually issued.

As we were preparing for a DC-3 project, we were involved with a government department which we would serve in developing isolated areas of the country. We felt this administration should request visas for the DC-3 crew. Instead, they advised us to go to the secretary general of the Ministry of Foreign Affairs, request them personally, and then send a follow-up letter.

We scheduled an appointment to see the secretary general with an official from the department involved. The main purpose was to present the needs of the DC-3 program. However, I also brought a letter requesting that our people be granted year-long visas. This was a long shot, a hope that I had nourished in prayer that the Lord would answer in this particular case. A request may be expedited through the bureaucracy if it can piggyback on another which may have fewer hurdles to surmount.

The result of that meeting? In four days our request for year-long visas had been granted. The chief of the Visa Department, who responds directly to the secretary general, said that we could start requesting year-long visas immediately. Pending visas under consideration would be granted on the same basis.

I Have a Great Idea

Richard Pittman

It is amazing to see how much good can be done if a person does not care who gets the glory for it. It was election time in a great South American republic. The candidates were out for votes. Obviously, to get them they had to have inspiring platforms. And they did. Nearly all included in their plans a bilingual education plank. They would teach Indian children to read first in their own mother tongue. Then they would use this skill as a basis for teaching Spanish. It was a popular idea—sure to win votes.

No one explained that the idea had reached the country through a gringo. And the gringo, Uncle Cam, was the last one to want them to explain. He was delighted that each aspirant put it forward as his own idea. That was a crucial part of its success.

I cannot recall how I came to realize that most missions (and missionaries) regard themselves as competitors with the governments of the countries in which they work. But it is surely true. Very few are prepared to allow the governments to be partners in the work they are doing. Still fewer are willing for the governments to get the glory for what they do. Only an infinitesimal number know how to ghostwrite the script for inspired government programs and remain anonymous afterward.

Uncle Cam was certainly one of the miniscule group. One of his secrets was his refusal to let past failures and discouragements cloud his vision or dull his enthusiasm. Another was his consummate care to make sure that officials of the host government got the glory for any noteworthy achievement, especially for having generated the idea in the first place.

Some object that if we look for guidance to government officials who are not of the same religious persuasion as we, we will be led in ways we do not want to go. But God has marvelously used such men on innumerable occasions to lead in ways which are clearly God's ways. Jim Dean, for example, often said to the director of Deccan College in India, "We would appreciate your guidance." He was never disappointed.

Not the least of our eminently satisfying activities in India was our relationship with that director. We continually sought his advice; he, with equal faithfulness, gave it.

Nor was his guidance in error. He told us to whom to relate in Delhi and how. He introduced us personally. He gave us a letter to the head of another large institution on the other side of India, who in turn introduced us to the collector of a large district in which we wanted to work. This man enabled us to start there.

Would it not have been better to ask the missions to guide us? No. However successful the missions might have been, God has made the government officials, not the missionaries, the stewards over the people and the land in which they live. We who seek to live and work there are dependent on the officials both for permission and for direction.

True, they sometimes sent us to the missionaries for advice. That is the way it worked in Irian Jaya. It is vital, however, to remember that we went to the officials first, and from them to the missionaries, with official blessing. It is also important to remember that we went not only to the Protestants but also to the Catholics. It is the way the government guided.

One day the most influential of the Catholic fathers drove up to our door with a rare, out-of-print book in his hand. "This book is not supposed to leave our library," he said, "but I know the government has asked you to study the languages of the Valley of the Tor. Reference materials about them are scarce. So we want to loan you this book, *The People of the Tor*."

It was the book we needed most!

Give Them a Piece of the Action

Richard Pittman

Daws Trotman, in the early days of the Navigators, was so sold on the faith principle that when a person asked how he could help, Daws would reply, "The Lord takes care of us." Finally one of his friends took him aside and said, "Daws, you won't let your friends know how they can help you. That is not right."

Daws took the message to heart and changed his ways. From then on, he let his friends know how they could help. Years ago I asked Uncle Cam why he asked the Mexican government officials for help. He said, "The main resource a politician has is power. Power can be used either for you or against you. The best way to keep it from being used against you is to get it started going for you."

How often we have had occasion to see the truth of that point of view! Even after a man leaves office or dies, as in the case of President Magsaysay, bureaucratic precedent and inertia take over. When his successor has to make decisions, it is far easier to do so on the basis of precedent than to try to be original. If the precedent was to help you, the odds are high that you will be helped again.

The path of least resistance in government work is to expect officials to do only what is required of them in the line of duty. To expect and seek only this much, however, may mean that they and we will fall far short of God's best for both. Since it is their country, and since much of what we are doing is really their responsibility, the government officials should be offered as many opportunities as possible to help in ways which are beyond the call of duty. The following are some examples:

A high official in Indonesia's Ministry of Education offered rides in his car from Bogor to Jakarta. These were gratefully accepted.

A Mexican official was told of the need for eucalyptus trees in Tetelcingo. He was delighted to make a contribution of a large number of seedlings.

Officials and scholars from several different countries were asked to make inquiries regarding the well-being and whereabouts of John and Carolyn Miller while they were being held. There was very good response from many.

The rector of Cenderawasih University invited Dick Pittman to be his house guest for several days; the invitation was gratefully accepted.

A former bishop of Kontum was asked to help locate the former Minister of Education of Cambodia and notify him that his wife and children were alive and well.

A former Minister of the Interior of South Vietnam was asked to help on legal matters relative to SIL property use in South Vietnam and gladly did so.

Very many present and former officials of a large number of countries have gladly given notes and letters of introduction when asked to do so.

Aaron Saenz, a distinguished Mexican leader, made several large contributions to the building of the SIL center in Tlalpan, Mexico.

Engineer Cuauhtemoc Cardenas, son of the late President Lazaro Cardenas, contributed architectural work in the planning and building at SIL Tlalpan.

Mrs. Magsaysay wrote an introduction to the biography of Gaspar Makil.

Rafael Ramirez, after questioning the use of Indian languages, contributed five dollars to the Townsends' garden in Tetelcingo. It did much to change his outlook. Distinguished citizens of many countries have gladly given time to serve on advisory councils in their respective countries.

When the Townsends were injured in a commercial plane crash in Chiapas, former President Cardenas marshaled all available help for them, including the state governor, in the plane which went to their aid.

Numerous officials, including several presidents and ambassadors, have participated in goodwill airplane ceremonies at home and abroad.

The total effect of these gestures has been to make them feel that the SIL work is their work, not a program of outsiders competing against them.

Of course there are boobytraps. One of the worst is to give the impression that it is a foreign project which is being helped, rather than a project of the host country which is being helped by the foreigner. In order to keep that misunderstanding from developing, it is important for expatriates, when they use first person plural pronouns (we, us, our, ours) in communications to national officials, to make sure these are understood as first person inclusive rather than exclusive. That is, the meaning must be perceived as "the project for which you and we are responsible" rather than "the project which we (foreigners) are running without your participation."

Even the naming of a project can make or break it. In Indonesia, for example, we talked a few times about the "Summer Institute of Linguistics-Cenderawasih University" project before we realized that it had to be "Cenderawasih University-Summer Institute of Linguistics" project.

Keep Them Informed

Ronald Gluck

When thirty orphaned vocational students came to Washington, DC, from Latin America, all members of the Ruiz family—Adelmo, Edelmira, Luisa, and Sammy—were involved in transporting, translating, and helping in many other ways. The country's ambassador to Washington, a special friend of Adelmo, was most appreciative.

After the students left Washington, Adelmo asked the ambassador to participate in the dedication send-off ceremony of a Piper Navajo twin engine plane. The ambassador agreed and took part in the program at the JAARS center in Waxhaw, North Carolina.

This ambassador is the former governor of a state which has about one-third of the country's Indian population. As governor he was the author of national legislation protecting all Indian lands and traditional forms of self-government. He has a great concern for the Indians.

"How is everything going for SIL in my country?" he asked Al Meehan, SIL branch director. Al briefly described our activities and opposition SIL was receiving there.

The ambassador already knew of SIL's special relationship with the former mayor of the capital city, who has been Minister of Education and a member of SIL's advisory committee. Now he instructed Al: "Maintain good contact with all politicians and the media. Keep them informed of SIL's activities. Indirectly you will have their support."

In a speech the ambassador said, "I like SIL's scientific and practical assistance to the Indians, but most of all I appreciate the spiritual motivation of Scripture translation behind your work. When your government signed the agreement with SIL, it was left open-ended so that you would have all the time you needed to complete your work. I am your friend and I am willing to help you either from Washington or in my country. I know where your opposition comes from. You need not worry about them."

The ambassador's comments reaffirmed the importance of being accountable to host governments. His government wants to see SIL succeed and expects SIL to be thorough in its government relations.

Tennis, Anyone?

John Strawser

As we bowed in prayer to thank God for sparing the lives of the crew in a crashed helicopter, I remembered how it had all begun with a tennis ball.

My family and I arrived at our overseas assignment in December 1989. We had not had a preference for a country in which to serve, but I had jokingly told the selection committee that I wanted to go where there was a Helio Courier and a tennis court!

Our first three months were spent learning the national language. Across from the university where we were staying were some tennis courts. I told my tutor about my love for tennis and found that the person with whom he lived played tennis regularly in the capital, an hour's drive away. My tutor introduced me to his friend, who in turn introduced me to the governor's club members with whom he played. I was invited to play and gradually became acquainted with many people, although I did not yet know what their work was. Later I found that most of them were prominent leaders in the province.

There were not enough tennis courts for all the players, so it was normal to play a set and then sit for a while. During this sitting time I studied the national language and culture and made many friends. These eventually opened doors to their homes and families and introduced us to other prominent people, thus leading us into everwidening circles of friends, crossing both social and political boundaries. As I completed my national language study and began work as a pilot, I continued to play at those same tennis courts, although less frequently.

When we moved to another city, I again found open doors to the national community through the tennis court. This time most of the players were military officers.

In May 1990 I represented our aviation department at an induction ceremony for a new commander of the air force base. An employee accompanied me to the ceremony, since my control of the national language was still imperfect. Upon arrival, I was amazed to discover that many of the dignitaries knew me. Now I could see them in uniform and identify their rank. I was introduced to the new commander by one of my tennis friends. He invited me to his tennis courts, and later that same week I played with him. It was the beginning of our strongest relationship.

Eventually other doors opened in the military community, but the one with the air force remained the strongest. I began to spend more and more time with those in the community, visiting in their homes with my family. We talked about many things, including the work of SIL. It was a good opportunity to help them to understand better that we were not there as a threat but to help their country. A few times I invited the local commanders to ride along on flights with me. It was these informal visits which laid the groundwork for our involvement in helping to find survivors of two downed helicopters.

As months passed, doors to meeting people in other cities were opened, as we saw our friends complete their assignments in one province and move to another. God has blessed and enriched our lives through our investment in relationships with the local people.

Dick, Make Me Look Good

Richard Pittman

The boss's boss was coming, and we expatriates were helping prepare for his arrival. The occasion was at least as important to us as it was to our sponsor because our visa applications had to be approved by the office of the visiting dignitary. Lacking his *vista bueno*, our applications could be delayed or even denied.

But the occasion was also important to our sponsor. He reported directly to this visiting official. His own rank, promotion, salary, budget, and staff depended on the good will of his superior. It was obviously important, therefore, to make as good an impression as possible.

Two SIL Helio Courier airplanes had been brought in for the day. There was also a helicopter in the project, but it was some distance away and would cost a fair bit in both effort and money to fly in. The pilots were understandably reluctant to make the extra investment. But the sponsor needed all the resources he could marshal to make his boss's visit memorable. "Dick, make me look good," he said to the SIL branch director, Dick Hugoniot. "Bring the helicopter in too." Dick hesitated a moment and then consented, making a mental note to economize in various places in order to find the $350 needed for the flight.

When the official arrived, SIL's sponsor proudly included, as a part of the tour, a review of the three aircraft. He invited the visitor to take a ride in the helicopter, initially without success. When Dick presently repeated the invitation, the educator, finally consenting, took his first helicopter ride. To the delight of everyone, it was a resounding success.

The visitor's enthusiasm was so substantial that both SIL and our sponsor benefited very much. The experience obviously contributed in a major way to the success of the visit.

"Bob," reported Dick Hugoniot to Bob Griffin later, "that was the best $350 I ever spent!" Relations with that office, once uncertain at best, were soon excellent.

Hams in the Equation

Allan Shannon, K3DSO/OA8S

One evening while working in the small Peruvian town of Ayacucho in the Andes Mountains, Don Burns, OA5AH, was talking to a ham friend of ours in Lima. We had never met Antonio but knew him through ham radio. As Don finished telling him about our work with the Quechuas in bilingual education, Antonio seemed deeply moved and told Don how much he appreciated the work of SIL and the help it was to his countrymen.

A week or so later Don and I had to go to Lima for a session of Congress which was discussing the Ministry of Education's bilingual education program for the highlands. Upon entering the hall of Congress, we heard the moderator ask, "And what is this budget for bilingual education?" Don tentatively raised a hand, saying, "I think I can explain, sir." At the sound of Don's voice the moderator shouted, "OA5AH?" in a loud voice; Don responded, "OA5JT?" It was Antonio! He immediately left the podium and ran down the aisle to embrace Don, much to the surprise of the other congressmen.

After the exchange of jargon that only hams understand, Antonio said, "Don, what brings you to Lima?"

"That budget for bilingual education that you just mentioned. Remember, it is what we talked about on the radio the other evening."

"Well, if that is what it is for, say no more. It is approved." Needless to say, Don and I floated out of Congress praising the Lord.

One of our fellows who had just finished a delightful conversation with another Peruvian ham, Fernando, looked up his address in the callbook to send him a QSL card (verification of radio contact). Much to his chagrin, he discovered the address to be the presidential palace; he had been speaking to the president of Peru! Paul Wyse, OA8V, finished with a contact and realized he had just talked with King Hussein of Jordan! The Peruvian hams know all our fellows, know they are with SIL, and always ask me about them when I am on the air.

But one of the biggest complaints from the Peruvian hams is that the missionaries seem to want a Peruvian license only to talk to the U.S.; they ignore, for the most part, the national hams. Since missionaries usually live in isolated areas of the country, the nationals want to contact them for QSL purposes but find that most of them do not respond.

To counteract this, our hams in Peru have been told to try to make at least three contacts on the national level for every one outside the country. Every new member who gets his license also gets a four-page glossary from us in Spanish, a list of all the ham jargon used locally with typical conversations, etc., which helps him to launch out. Down through the years our members have formed hundreds of solid relationships with government and military leaders and influential businessmen alike.

Maintaining government and public relations is everybody's job. If we say we have come to serve, let us serve by getting involved with the nationals in radio clubs, nets, giving technical help, etc. Paul Wyse is a good example. He has stimulated contacts on RITTY, OSCAR, and the use of the higher bands of six and two meters. Over the past eighteen years I have serviced hundreds of radios for nationals, taught courses in radio, etc. I can hardly get on the air without some ham wanting to consult with me about technical questions and problems with his equipment. SIL has hardly scratched the surface of this most valuable tool of public relations called ham radio.

Just before leaving Peru I dropped in on an old friend who visited our people at Yarinacocha with his family. He is now the director general of telecommunications of Peru! As I left his office he said, "Allan, if your people need any help in communications, like licenses or frequencies, the door is always open. Have them come directly to me."

So if our motto is service, let us not overlook radio communication. Instead, let it be a tool of service to our host country and God will bless it as He has all the other aspects of our work.

A Bear Hug in the Soviet Embassy

David Witmer

Recently my wife and I had the opportunity to glean some principles of government relations work from a predecessor in the Washington liaison office. Les Troyer stressed some of the following as being crucial to the work:

Pray about everything at all times.

Develop a love for the people with whom you are working.

Be willing to take the servant's role, even when it is the hardest thing to do.

Be able to converse well in small talk.

Maintain general disassociation from home country diplomats and their counterparts, in order to show more of an international orientation.

Demonstrate sincerity and patience in your relationships; faking it will show up eventually.

Learn to keep your mouth shut and listen; it pays off.

Use your imagination to make and keep contacts; cultivate those relationships.

Recognize individuals through letters, including sending copies of good press articles about those individuals.

Remember birthdays.

If blunders occur, confess and correct them as quickly as possible.

Send letters of congratulations on new appointments; send New Year's cards.

Be a part of the cocktail circuit if possible (one official stated to Les, "You people must really be important because I see you at all these functions").

When dealing with each individual, ask yourself what kind of needs this person has; seek ways of meeting these needs.

Love each one. Uncle Cam said, "If you hold him in your arms and hold him tight, he cannot hit you very hard."

Our time closed with a story which Les related based on an experience he once had when Uncle Cam was in town:

The agenda of the day called for a visit to the Soviet embassy. Uncle Cam was wearing his big Stetson as usual and Les was accompanying him. They entered the embassy and almost immediately a voice called out, "Uncle Cam!" A big burly fellow appeared and engulfed Uncle Cam in a bear hug in which Uncle Cam all but disappeared. Uncle Cam then proceeded to pull out a copy of *The Christian Herald* and draw the man's attention to it. He explained, "My father read this magazine when I was a boy and it now has a circulation of 250,000. In this issue is an article I wrote about my recent trip to your beautiful country."

When Uncle Cam offered the article to the man to read, he accepted it and asked if he could make a copy. He disappeared and after ten or fifteen minutes reappeared. Throughout the visit and discussion of the article, Uncle Cam emphasized the good qualities of the Russian people and countryside. He said nothing about the government of Russia. When he told about his father's reading the magazine and of the circulation number, he communicated two things: (1) that the magazine has been around a long time and is not a new creation; and (2) that it was not just a small issue but very widespread in its readership. This helped give credibility to what Uncle Cam was hoping to accomplish.

C.

Be affectionately respectful to soldiers and police.

Chat Them Up!

Robert Griffin

Chat them up! That is what I was doing when I drank coffee with Philippine friends in the ready room at an air force base. Lt. Saavedra, a young supply officer to whom I reported at six-month intervals, became a good friend. One day he proudly showed me photos of his wife and four children. I could guess what his life was like on a lieutenant's pay, so I said to him, as is the custom in the Philippines, "Lt. Saavedra, for you life must be very hard."

"Oh, yes, Mr. Bob, life is very hard."

"Then what you need is my little moneymaker." (I frequently carried pocket tricks with me.) I reached in my pocket and pulled out a couple of brass cylinders and a brass ring. I said, "Lieutenant, if you use this properly it will produce money for you. Abraca-dabra. Look! Four nickels—twenty cents! That was easy, wasn't it? Now, we stack them up and put this ring around them, and, abracadabra, just as quickly they are gone—disappeared. Isn't that your trouble? When money comes it goes just as fast."

His eyes got bigger and bigger as he followed my every move. "Do it again!" he said. I've always been told a major rule for a magician is never to repeat a magic trick, but for him I did it again. Totally amazed, he called to the thirty-some officers at their desks all over the room: "Hey, you guys, come over here; I want to show you something." They all crowded around. I did it once more, and then before they could ask to see it again I fled. The lieutenant never forgot that trick. Every six months he asked, "Bob, do you have your moneymaker?"

"I don't have it today," I sometimes answered, "but I have my finger guillotine." When I used this trick one time at a dinner table, the hostess got up and left. She was sure I'd get blood all over the tablecloth!

When that trick became old, I used a dexterity test, one that a friend, an industrial arts teacher in Spokane, Washington, made for me. It is a block of wood with a hole drilled in it and one end plugged. The plug holds a small piece of rubber band that loops inside the hole. You tell your unsuspecting friend to carefully use the plunger with the little hook carved in it, catch the rubber band, and snap it. What you don't say is that it is impossible. The only way to "snap" it is to let the plunger slip quickly from your fingers. It is an intriguing puzzle, and one seldom solved. However, there is no "magic" to it.

All these were little icebreakers, easy means of relating to the officers. Larry Montgomery taught me the value of pocket tricks. Diplomats, officers, everyone is always interested.

Ambassador Sir Paulias Matane was intrigued by my money-maker. I invited him to attend the dedication of a Cessna, the gift of friends from Central Lynn, Oregon, for the work in Papua New Guinea. He was a new ambassador, Papua New Guinea's first to the U.S. I met him with the Cessna when he flew to Portland, Oregon, and we flew together to Central Lynn where we landed on a farmer's grass strip. We spent a week there in the home of a farm family. After two days the ambassador began to visibly relax, kicking off his shoes as soon as he got in the door. "I would feel even better if I could take my socks off," he said one day with a grin. It was there, sitting around the kitchen table visiting, that I first showed him my moneymaker. He was fascinated and pestered me for days to show him how it worked. He enjoyed those days; everyone was so warm and welcoming. He loved it.

"Bob," he said one day, "I have to tell you, I came to America with a chip on my shoulder because I met antagonism toward the U.S. in India, Africa, everywhere I traveled." He had encountered this attitude during years of travel as an education official in PNG.

Then later he was appointed ambassador to the U.S., Canada, Mexico, and the UN, and had been in his current position only three months. "In the months I have been here," he said, "I haven't seen anything in Washington, in Mexico City, in Toronto, or in New York to cause me to change my mind about the impressions of the U.S. that I brought with me—until now. I'm so impressed with these people in Oregon, loving people, kind, and open."

"Mr. Ambassador, please remember that what you are seeing in Oregon represents about 98% of America," I explained. From then on, his attitude toward America was very different. We built a warm and lasting friendship. But Sir Paulias still wonders how my moneymaker works!

Where Are They?

An SIL pilot

Crashed on the mountainside—but where? It was no surprise to me that a helicopter being operated by the air force of the host nation in which we served had been caught in a strong downdraft near a 15,400-foot mountain peak and had plummeted to earth at 11,500 feet. I had recently flown through that same pass myself. If I had not done a quick 180-degree turn out of the downdraft, I too would have smashed into the face of the mountain.

Even though the downed helicopter had radio contact, no one could locate it or the crew the first two days after the crash. Now, thirty-four hours after its disappearance, the commander called for SIL to come to a rescue meeting. He and his colleagues expanded the search plan, encouraging our involvement and suggestions.

As final plans were being made and the meeting was ending, I approached the commander. "Do you have any more thoughts?" he asked.

"Yes," I said, "I think we should close with a time of prayer."

"Good," he agreed, "I'll announce it and you lead."

"The one to lead us," I replied, "should be our chief pilot. He is the ranking person in our operation."

The next morning the chief pilot and I were the first to leave the airport. However, an air force Boeing 737 reached the general area before we did. The downed crew heard them and sent up a weak radio signal. As we approached the crash site, we could see the crew in their orange flight suits waving their arms. Behind the downed aircraft was a signal fire, barely visible because of the high winds and turbulence. As we led the rescue helicopter to the site, I videoed the action. It seemed miraculous that all survived the crash with very little injury.

Back at the airport, after we had all gathered in the crew room, the commander spoke. He thanked all involved and asked us of SIL to lead in prayer, thanking God for guiding us. The rescued pilot and copilot gave me their crash compass and signal mirror as souvenirs. I gave them a letter that I had prepared the night before to throw to the crew of the downed chopper, plus a keychain with a Scripture verse on it.

Soon after that eventful day most of those involved in the rescue came to our house to view the video I had made. We then realized that if the helicopter had gone down fifty meters to the left, it would have rolled down a steep embankment and all would have been lost.

We also realized that the strong friendship and trust the air force and SIL felt for each other had been major factors in making this rescue possible.

Lost Crash Site

An SIL pilot

I had just returned to the hangar after a disappointing day. It was 3:30 p.m. and our Helio Courier mission had not been accomplished.

One of my air force friends was waiting at the parking pad. Had I heard the news? No. An air force helicopter had gone down in the jungle just minutes away from the airport. Could I help look for it?

After talking with the commanding officer and our two senior pilots, I agreed to go. Not much daylight was left. A national trainee was assigned to the right seat and four air force men, who were also friends, took the back seats. Before I could suggest it myself, one of the men in the back seat asked me to pray. I did so.

An air force Puma helicopter had been searching for four hours without success. Seven minutes before we reached its location, however, they radioed that the lost chopper had been found. I started to return to the airport, but Dave, my aviation manager, came on the air recommending I go back to the site in order to pinpoint its precise location with our global positioning system. At the same time the pilot of the Puma came on the air again. He called, "I have lost the site and need your help."

Again I reversed course and flew back. Crisscrossing the ridge where we believed it to be, my national copilot soon spotted the crash. Since I had global positioning site equipment, we were able to list coordinates for the location; the Puma was soon able to lift the survivors out. I followed the Puma back. My copilot and I cried and prayed with the air force men who had lost their copilot and friend in the crash.

The next day I loaned our GPS equipment to the Puma helicopter to enable it to relocate the site and airlift out the dead copilot. In response to an air force request, we were able later to obtain and deliver to them GPS equipment of their own.

Ready for the Earthquake?

Kenneth Wiggers and Richard Pittman

A Helio Courier airplane is ideal for the rugged terrain of Irian Jaya, where long airstrips are rarely possible. Some visionaries, therefore, both in Indonesia and out, believed that Cenderawasih University and the Summer Institute of Linguistics could launch a flying program with a Helio Courier which would greatly benefit the inaccessible peoples of Irian Jaya's remote interior.

Numerous donors believed the vision, gave money for the airplane, and paid to transport it to Papua New Guinea. Ken and

Pat Wiggers trusted God to provide the documentation to bring the plane into Indonesia and proceeded to PNG to wait.

The wheels of bureaucracy grind slowly. Though they arrived in Port Moresby May 5, 1976, neither visas nor an important permit were immediately forthcoming. It looked as though they might be in for a long wait.

But on June 25 disaster struck. An earthquake of gigantic proportions buried whole villages in the trackless interior of Irian Jaya. The combined resources of the government of Indonesia and the Missionary Aviation Fellowship were insufficient to cope with destruction of that magnitude.

On July 2 a radiogram crackled through the ether: "Indonesian Civil Aviation officials request you come and bring the Helio Courier airplane. A temporary pilot's license and permission to use the aircraft will be provided."

Were Ken and Pat ready? On July 3 Ken arrived in Sentani with the Helio Courier. Pat and their son Dirk arrived on July 7. Many weeks of emergency flying lay ahead of them, exhausting but gratifying because of the consciousness that when the call came they were prepared.

Attention on Top of a Norseman

Merrill Piper

In the '50s I was flying a Norseman airplane in the northern part of the Peruvian jungle. On one trip I had to land for fuel on the Ucayali River near Iquitos, at the headwaters of the Amazon. I taxied up to the military center called Base Itaya. The men came down to greet me and help unload the airplane, as they normally did, for I had numerous friends there by that time. My flight plans required that I spend the night in Iquitos. Early the next morning I came out to refuel the aircraft so that I could take off shortly after sunup.

I was standing on top of the Norseman, a big single-engine airplane, refueling it five gallons at a time as the military men handed me containers of gasoline. As I did this I became vaguely aware of a commotion at the parade ground directly in front of me. A soldier touched my pant leg and pointed toward the activity; then I realized that they were playing the national anthem and raising their flag for the day.

I instantly stiffened to attention and faced the flag-raising ceremony. At its completion I was astonished to see the men on the parade ground flock over to shake my hand! They wanted to express their appreciation for my having recognized their country, their flag, and their national anthem. Even the commander of the base came to thank me. From then on, everyone in the compound, from the commander down, came to shake my hand every time I arrived.

Some time later I had occasion to spend a number of weeks in Iquitos making ferry trips from Base Itaya out to a jungle area where several translators were working. It was not unusual on those flights to bring back a sick person or an expectant mother. Everyone at the base was quite aware of how often this took place.

One morning I landed at Base Itaya after spending the night at a village with one of our translators. As I taxied up to the dock, the commander came toward me, waving a newspaper. He was obviously upset. Finally, speaking in English so that I could better understand him, he exclaimed, "Look, Captain, at what they are saying about you and your friends in the jungle! These are all lies! They say that you are our enemies and we are to fear you! I have witnessed with my own eyes all the good things you have done. You bring in anyone who is sick; you care for him and help him. I am here to say that you are our friend!"

Another time I was spending several days at Iquitos and needed to contact Yarinacocha. It was urgent. I decided to go to the commander at Base Itaya, about a ten-minute taxi ride from my lodging, to see if he could help me.

The commander greeted me with a warm smile and hand-shake, asking what he could do for me. After I explained, he said, without hesitation, "Go to the sergeant in charge of radio communications. Tell him I said it is OK for you to talk to Yarinacocha."

When I approached the sergeant, he immediately stopped what he was doing and tuned in Yarinacocha on the radio. I took care of my business and thanked the young man for his help.

Some time later a companion who was with me in Iquitos needed to talk to Yarinacocha; he wondered if there was a way to make contact. I said, "Let's go out to Base Itaya and see." We went to the room on top of a high hill where radio operations were conducted. Again the sergeant interrupted his work to greet me. I introduced him to my friend and asked if it were possible, at his convenience, to contact Yarinacocha. "Right away!" responded the young man, twisting dials. In a few minutes Yarinacocha was on the line and my companion transmitted his message.

He was amazed to see how spontaneously this young soldier had met our request. The sergeant had a genuine interest in what we were doing in his country; our friendship was real.

Key to a Turnaround

Merrill Piper

"Why did you bring corn? We wanted rice," complained the officers.

I had been in Ecuador about a year as an SIL pilot. Part of my work included making flights for the Ecuadorian military from Shell Mera to the jungle. We had a contract to fly supplies for them. I was happy to do this, realizing that my help would show the government that we were sincere in saying that we wanted to serve them in every way possible.

After a number of months of making three or four flights a week to a certain base, it began to irritate me that I never seemed to bring the right thing! Officers at my destination always complained that instead of rice, they wanted corn, or if I brought corn, they wanted rice. They grumbled that I never brought what they had ordered. My patience was beginning to wear thin.

One night, after a particularly unpleasant encounter with the lieutenant, I asked the Lord, "What should I do? What am I doing wrong?" Slowly it dawned on me that I was trying to please men rather than God. I quietly prayed, "Lord, forgive me. From now on my goal will be to please You and to honor Your name."

The next day I loaded supplies onto the plane and flew to the usual location. To my astonishment, the lieutenant greeted me with a smile, shaking my hand warmly, and said, "Thank you, Captain!" I was dumbfounded; this was the first time he had ever thanked me! On my second trip that day, he gave me a gift of two chickens to take home. I was overwhelmed. How good it was to be reminded that a sincere desire to serve others in the name of the Lord can be the key to a complete turnaround in difficult situations.

Ten Cheeses for the Captain

David Farah and Richard Pittman

"A man's gift maketh room for him." (Proverbs 18:16) "And Jesse said unto David his son, … carry these ten cheeses unto the captain of their thousand, and look how thy brethren fare." (I Samuel 17:17-18)

The translator of a well-known English version used the word "bribe" in the proverb quoted above, then hedged it with a footnote to the effect that, while this is often the case, it is not to be practiced.

But gifts and bribes are not the same. They may, in fact, be diametrically different. Sentimental gifts especially, such as flowers, an autographed personal picture, fruit, or a meaningful souvenir, may have little financial value but they do represent a serious effort made by the giver to please and bless the receiver.

A sentimental gift can cost the giver much more in time, thought, and effort than a bribe. But the result is also infinitely more worthwhile than a bribe. It builds esteem, gratitude, good memories. And it opens doors. It enabled David to see his brothers with their commanding officer's blessing and ultimately gave him the opportunity for the confrontation with Goliath.

Help from the Sidelines

Lester Troyer

We had first met this air force officer at an official reception in Manila. It was a "high-powered" affair, of the kind where everyone who was anyone was there—including a few like us who were "nobodies." He was a colonel in the Philippine Air Force and was standing off on the sidelines either looking bored or trying to cover his feelings of insecurity at such a "bash." When we first began going to such parties, Madeline and I had felt led by the Lord to look for junior officials and others who seemed ill at ease. We then introduced ourselves and tried to make friends. We might rescue the evening for such a person. After all, we had nothing to lose, since we were not social climbers.

We found him not insecure but bored with the party and ready for our friendship and conversation. We enjoyed him and met him several times later during that season. Then we lost track of him for a year or two. The country went through elections and a change of presidents. With the incoming new administration there was a shift of top officers in the air force, and one morning the headlines of the city newspapers informed us that our colonel friend, who had been promoted previously to general, had just been appointed commanding officer of the Philippine Air Force.

About six months later one of our planes had an accident in the mountains of northern Luzon. Our people were able to get the wings out of the mountains with the help of dedicated mountain people. Our JAARS pilots flew the engine out with another plane. But the fuselage remained staked down to the terrace alongside the remote mountain airstrip. We wanted badly to salvage that plane; we went to the U.S. ambassador's office pleading for one of the big U.S. flying cranes that were stationed at one of the bases. Our men knew that would do the trick. But it was of no use. Consent was not given.

We were a bit reluctant to impose ourselves on the Philippine Air Force since we were not sure they had the kind of equipment needed. But our JAARS men finally decided we should try.

Since I had met the general when he was still a colonel, I was elected to meet with him and see if the air force would be willing to help us get the plane out of the mountains. It was a sultry morning when I called at the general's staff headquarters. I approached the general's aide-de-camp with my request for an appointment. He was a salty major. Without even looking at his appointment book he informed me coldly and officially that I would have to wait at least a week, if not longer. "The general is very busy these days with military matters!" So that was that.

I was nonplused. He seemed very unbending, very proper in his manner, and not inclined to discuss the matter further. I sat in front of his desk pondering the situation and had just risen to leave, when in walked the general with an entourage of lesser officers in tow.

"Hello there, Troyer! I haven't seen you for a long time. How have you been? Come in, come in. What can we do for you?"

I got a glimpse of the major's look of utter surprise and some chagrin as I followed the general and his officers into his office. I was able to convey our congratulations to him on his appointment (as we had done earlier by letter) and then get down to business. When I left his office fifteen minutes later, we had the promise of one of their large helicopters to lift our downed Helio from its stricken condition in the mountains. To make a long story short, we got the plane out, and it resumed flying service in the Philippines.

D.

Call on diplomats.

Cultivate the Diplomatic Corps

Cameron Townsend

The first day we were in Washington we called at several embassies. We were particularly pleased with the reception given by the ambassador from India. He is new. He had been vice-chancellor of Delhi University. He seems to be an outstanding man, and he is appreciative of our interest in the languages of his country.

The ambassador from Indonesia was especially attentive. He brought in three heads of departments of the embassy to listen, and we had a good visit with him.

There are now two ambassadors from Papua New Guinea, one for Washington and one for the UN. Bud Hancock set up a dinner engagement with them at the Chinese restaurant they had selected. He had a very pleasant time with them.

We had a good visit also with Ambassador Bindzi of the Cameroon embassy. When I told him that one of our couples had been denied an entrance permit, he said, "Oh, that's understandable, because we feel that foreign organizations should use our own citizens in every way they can." I tried to explain to him that our people do not receive salaries. We go out just to serve, and the linguists need the help of people who understand their program when it comes to management, offices, etc.

We need to find ways to be given a different classification in the eyes of the countries where we serve. We are not an organization that comes in to do a host government's job, but an organization that has come to serve the people of the country where unwritten languages are spoken, to help, to make a contribution, to leave behind dictionaries and grammars, and to cultivate good will. We need to make it plain that we are not paid salaries for this work, so that they will not feel that salaries which they suppose we get should go to nationals. If the nationals want to work without salaries, like the person whose immigration permit is turned down, that is fine; but of course they do not.

Thursday was the National Prayer Breakfast, with some three thousand people eating together. The day before, there was a special breakfast for the vice-president. There I had a chance to talk with Ambassador Dobrynin and tell him how we want to feature the alphabet from Armenia, as well as the one from Georgia, in the Museum of the Alphabet. They are the oldest in the USSR, going back, I believe, to the fourth century A.D. Dobrynin was sitting next to Billy Graham, but Billy had not arrived yet, so I had the ambassador's ear for a few moments. He is the dean of the diplomatic corps, having been there longer than any other ambassador.

We had a wonderful time with the ambassador from Mexico, not only at one of the dinners, but also at his office. He was enthusiastic and favorable toward us. He said he had talked with the president's private secretary, Dr. Casillas, half an hour earlier, and that he had told Casillas we would be coming in a few minutes. Casillas had said, "Greet them for me." He seems to be the man the president has designated to take care of our visa needs in Mexico.

I am very much concerned about our developing and continuing to put emphasis on our contacts with ambassadors in Washington. They need to understand us. They need to be shown courtesies. I appreciate what is being done in Washington by our limited staff there.

I hope it will work out so we can bring more of them to visit JAARS. I believe that the Museum of the Alphabet is going to help a great deal.

Little Duster among Cadillacs

Lester Troyer

The afternoon had been hot and dry as a charcoal sketch. Dragging myself home on the crowded bus into Arlington, Virginia, I wanted nothing more than to sit in the backyard under the big, old maple tree and soak up the evening's solitude. I wanted to be away from people, from the urban rush of Washington, DC, and from the noise of the city. But in my briefcase was an invitation from an African embassy with whom we had not had much contact. I had befriended an attache earlier by getting him some linguistic information which was useful to him in his office. He was surprisingly grateful, profusely so. This was the night when the embassy celebrated their national independence day. Independence from what, I was not sure. I knew that I should go, but I was carrying on a dialogue with the Lord.

I assumed that the attache was the only person at the party who would notice Madeline and me. I had never met the ambassador. I had had a hard, hot day at the office. I needed my rest. And besides that, I was weary of always parking the little green Plymouth Duster six blocks away from these receptions on Embassy Row lest sometime (and it almost happened once) I get caught in the long line of low, sleek limousines purring up to the party gates. I didn't feel up to going through that hassle just to be seen walking around in my old, shiny, dark blue suit, drinking soft drinks, smiling and mixing with the nobility and making small talk. Surely the Lord understood! Right?

Wrong! The Lord told me He loved me very much, but He also told me, as He has many others down through history, "Get up and go about the Kingdom business. The day may come when you will not have the opportunity." So I pried myself out of the lawn chair, showered, combed my hair, polished my shoes, put on the old blue suit, got into the battered Duster, and sailed away for Embassy Row in downtown Washington. Madeline was unable to come. Nearing the ambassadors' residences, I saw the Cadillacs and Lincolns gliding up the street. After hunting for ten minutes for a parking space, I finally found one on a side street four blocks away and "hoofed" it to the party.

It was a gala affair. Most of the glittering people from the local diplomatic corps were there along with some of Washington's finest. I proceeded through the reception line with the appropriate handshaking and into the garden where the party was in full progress. I made sure to meet the attache in reference, but he was preoccupied with a dignitary from his home country and barely recognized me. I moved around the room, meeting other diplomats who were friends of SIL and our Washington staff. Then I came to an ambassador from one of the countries in Africa whom we wanted to get to know better because of the SIL work there. He was friendly and talkative, more so than he had previously been.

"Mr. Troyer, you SIL people must be all right! I meet you and your people at so many of these diplomatic functions. Only people with a good reputation and good standing with the international community are invited to these affairs," he smiled. Our relationship was reinforced!

That made my evening. In fact, it did more than just make my evening; it made me ashamed before the Lord for thinking earlier of reasons why I should not have gone to the reception. I knew that the ambassador was right. Being seen in the right places is very important to the diplomatic world; it makes a statement. I also knew that there were people in Washington who would have given their eyeteeth to be at such a reception simply because it would have been a status builder for them and their businesses.

I confessed my weakness to the Lord and renewed my determination to attend all such functions, even though the flesh sometimes is weak. I know that the Lord provides ample funds of strength and fortitude to park the Duster out of the way in order not to impede the high-powered traffic of Cadillacs and Lincolns so we can be about the Lord's business—even on Embassy Row!

The Only Children in the Crowd

Richard Hugoniot

One of the universals on Planet Earth is to pay your respects to high officials once a year. The time to do it in Indonesia is *Idul Fetri*, an Islamic holiday. Our Indonesian friends told us that the governor of Irian Jaya held open house on that day and that we should go to greet him with our children.

Dressed in our Sunday-go-to-meeting best, we piled into the jeep, only to discover we had a flat tire. Back into the house I charged, changed clothes, changed the tire (generating grime and sweat), returned to the house to bathe and put on good clothes again. We arrived at the governor's mansion at 7 p.m.

As we came into the reception hall we found ourselves in a large crowd of finely dressed guests eyeing a table groaning with good food as they waited for the governor to appear. We were the only expatriates, and ours were the only children.

Ruefully wondering how to retreat, I discovered it was too late. The governor and his wife came in just then and looked our way. Recognizing us from their visit to our center at Danau Bira and noticing the children, they broke into big smiles. Coming straight to us, they greeted us warmly, took us personally to the laden table, and made us guests of honor for the lovely meal. The experience helped cement a most meaningful relation with both of them throughout their term of office.

The Best Cookie I Never Tasted

David Witmer

Ron Gluck and I recently went to visit the ambassador of an African nation on his birthday. Conflicting schedules had prohibited us from an earlier gathering. We had determined to take a cake but ended up with one of those enormous pizza-sized cookies that had "Happy Birthday, Mr. Ambassador" written in chocolate icing on its face.

We arrived on time and were ushered in. The ambassador immediately asked what was in the large box Ron was carrying. Ron set it down and opened it to reveal the chocolate chip contents, drawing the ambassador's attention to the writing on the cookie. "Oh, thank you!" exclaimed the ambassador. Ron lit the single candle that adorned the cookie's face, and after a few moments the ambassador bent and blew it out. I picked up the bag of plates, napkins, and forks we had brought with us in order to share in the celebration. "If I had known," he said, "I would have invited my staff to come and join us; however, I will have them join me later." With that, he closed the box and gestured to us to sit down. The paper plates and plastic forks went unused.

The next forty-five minutes were spent catching up on everyone's activities and looking to the future. The ambassador excitedly talked about a couple, his close friends, whom he was helping to sponsor financially during a tour of his country. We could tell this was of much importance to him because of his great desire for this couple to see his church in his home village; Ron told me later that this is a strong traditional value in Africa, for one to lay out the best he has for his friends. Since the ambassador could not be there in person, he was providing for his friends during their visit to his home. He had also arranged for the tour of his country to include a visit to the SIL center in the capital.

We talked about his son who had just finished a study program at Cambridge—the first Penn State doctoral candidate to be accepted by Cambridge for partial study. The ambassador was elated at his son's achievements academically as well as in music and sports. His son had since gone to meet his mother in Paris, then flown on with her to their home in Africa in order to welcome the ambassador's friends upon their arrival.

The ambassador then asked about our child who was due to be born just six days before. I regretted having to break the news that the child had been stillborn but was able to share with him that we did not send a general announcement, preferring to share the news individually as opportunity presented itself. At first it appeared that he was insulted at not being told, but after the explanation he understood. I believe that is another example of our need to understand his culture; the extended family includes friends, even from other cultures, and there is a desire to share burdens as well as joys.

He then mentioned that he and his wife would be in their home nation on leave during December and January. I asked if his village was near that of another friend whom Robin and I planned to visit on our way to the Africa Orientation Course in January. He said, "Only one hour away! Plan on being our guests for a short while when you come." Ron asked the ambassador if he would be willing to speak at the course, and the ambassador readily consented.

Invitations seemed to flow freely to one another's homes; my parents (who had hosted the ambassador and his family last November in Pennsylvania), Ron and Ruth, Robin and I were all included. He shared with us that a shift was going to take place within the diplomatic corps of his country and that he might be reassigned. We expressed our hope that he not be moved, and he himself stated his wish either to remain in the U.S. or to return to his own country. Friends have to be developed every time you move, he said, and God had given him some beautiful ones here, including those who bring him birthday cookies. Then, too, there is the need to move everything, from suitcases to pots and pans, and he has had enough of that in the past twelve years of being away from home.

We prepared to leave and thanked him for his graciousness in receiving us. As we started toward the door, he closed it and asked Ron to pray for the three of us. This is the first time I have ever experienced this sort of action on the part of an ambassador.

And so we left without even a bite of that scrumptious-looking cookie; I had thought such a nibble would suffice for lunch that day. As we went down the stairs, saying goodbye to the secretaries and receptionist, however, I found the contentment of the Lord satisfying me completely. After we had crossed the street I turned to Ron and said, "That was the best cookie I never tasted!"

The Lare Family Move

Steven Jacobsen

Attache Lare from the embassy of Togo in Washington had to move his family of six from their one-bedroom apartment to a larger one he had found. As a stranger in America, he had not realized that he must give notice at the old apartment; he found himself owing rent at two places and financially unable to rent a truck to make the move. He called me in desperation, and I prayed with him. We asked the Lord to help us find a truck we could borrow and a way to avoid paying two rents.

Finding a truck proved fruitless, until God sent an old Navigator buddy, Fraser Bennett, now an SILer, to the office. He asked me what I was up to, and I explained the situation briefly. It just so happened that his family had a truck and it was available! Not only did Fraser offer his truck but also his services; the Lares were overjoyed to see us.

Immediately we began grabbing furniture for the first load. I was a little surprised to find none of Lare's coworkers from the embassy, but Lare, his three young boys, Fraser, and I accomplished the move in three loads and six hours.

Lare was stunned that I would help him and overwhelmed that Fraser would spend six hours moving a complete stranger! When assured that we would not accept money, he said to Fraser, "You don't even know me, and yet you help me for six hours. I pray God that He will bless you for the kindness you have shown me and my family. I do not understand why you would do this for me, a stranger from Africa."

Then Lare asked us, "For six hours you have worked together as if you were brothers; why?" We were happy to explain Jesus' two commands to him: "Thou shalt love the Lord thy God with all thy heart, and with all thy soul, and with all thy mind. Thou shalt love thy neighbor as thyself."

Later Lare told me, "You are no longer just my friend; you are my brother. I will tell everyone in the embassy about you and your friend Fraser and how you helped me too much!" The privilege was ours. We are unworthy servants; we have only done our duty.

First Passenger in Cameroon

Ronald Gluck, Kent Hirschelman, and Richard Pittman

I knew that my first passenger would, in African eyes, be an omen—for good or bad luck. It was with unusual interest, therefore, that I shook the outstretched hand of the first Cameroonian to fly with me in his fatherland.

"My name is Solomon, Mr. Gluck," he smiled, cracking my knuckles in his great grip. "I knew one of your men at the University of Michigan."

"You did?" I replied with surprise. "Who was that?"

"Professor Kenneth Pike of the English Department."

"How did you happen to meet him?"

"I was there to learn English. There were no English classes on Sunday, but I was told he led a discussion, in English, of the lives of men like Joseph, Daniel, David, and Job. I joined the discussions."

Ruth and I entertained Solomon and his wife Virginia in our home in Arlington. Years later one of his kidneys failed so badly that he was told his only hope was a transplant. With no money to pay for such a costly procedure, he returned home to die. But he did not die—Cameroonian Christians prayed for him and he was healed. The result? He became the prime motivator in Cameroon's National Prayer Breakfast movement.

In the spring of 1995 SIL's Kent and Suzanne Hirschelman of the Philippine branch attended the Third International Workshop of the National Institutions for the Promotion and Protection of Human Rights.

"Hi," greeted another delegate. "My name is Solomon... Solomon Nfor Gwei of Cameroon. You are with SIL? I know the Pikes and Glucks. I was Ron's first passenger when he started the SIL flying program in my country. It became the airline of choice for our president."

There is a respected voice in Cameroon, constantly urging forgiveness and reconciliation in the spirit of Christ among numerous political leaders and factions. He is chairman of the Human Rights Commission. Name? Solomon Nfor Gwei.

A Narrow Escape

David Presson

Weeks before the ceremony which was to celebrate the twenty-fifth anniversary of the start of SIL work in Ivory Coast, I had all details in place...so I thought. The mayor of Abidjan had offered to lend us, free of charge, the big tent and chairs we needed for the occasion. The Minister of Higher Education and Scientific Research, under whom we serve, had happily agreed to be guest of honor and featured speaker.

Then...disaster. A major political rally was organized for the same day and time as our event. The tent and chairs which had been promised to us were preempted for the rally. And the minister who had promised to address our audience was obliged to commit himself to the political meeting instead.

Trying to stifle my anger, I stomped out of the office. What should I do? In turmoil I went to the mayor's services department, which is near the SIL center. The gentleman in charge of setting up equipment was already aware of my problem and told me that he wanted to help. He informed me that private services could provide the installation we needed. I explained that I did not know prices or how to go about arranging details. Without a second of thought he said, "I'll do all that for you. I have a truck to pick up the tent and chairs. If I order them, the cost will not be much."

My anxieties were quickly stilled as I learned that the price was indeed very reasonable. Why, I wondered, would this man whom I had never met go to all that trouble for me? So I asked. "Before we had a phone in our office," he replied, "I came regularly to your center to make my phone calls. Had it not been for your helpfulness to me, I could not have done my work."

But we still had to replace the guest-of-honor/principal speaker. Providentially the minister had thought of that and had appointed the Director of Higher Education to take his place. I had not previously met this man, so I went with some trepidation to arrange details for his visit. To my astonishment he greeted me by asking about the health of Bob Cruzen and Albert Veenkamp. How did he happen to know the names of our computer department manager and his technician?

"Oh," he explained, reading my mind, "my computer was malfunctioning. I simply asked for their help without drawing attention to my title. In fact, I called on them several times. They were very helpful. I feel that speaking at your ceremony is not just a public duty but also a privileged private opportunity for me to extol SIL's accomplishments."

The celebration was a huge success. But I shivered as I thought how easily it could have been otherwise. Some unavailable SIL administrator could have refused to let an outsider use the SIL phone. Or some overworked computer technician could have denied the request of an unknown stranger for help with his broken computer because he was too busy!

"Help us, Lord," I prayed, "never to yield to the self-serving instincts which would have turned away those two men, rejecting the SIL commitment of service to all!"

A Great Idea Came into Your Head

Cameron Townsend

It is wonderful how the Lord touched the heart of the ambassador of Panama when UNESCO gave us, in Washington, an award for literacy. The ambassador came to the ceremony and was won over to the work we are doing.

At first he did not believe in using vernacular languages for the first stages of instruction. But the Soviet ambassador had sent a representative who sat at the same table as the ambassador from Panama. They were close enough to be able to converse. The Soviet representative had been born and raised in an area of the Soviet Union where they had their own local language, just as Indian groups of Panama have their own languages. His government had arranged for bilingual education so that he could start his studies—first grade, second grade, and third grade—in his own mother tongue, and then shift to the national language. Then God arranged for this man from the Soviet Union to convince the ambassador from Panama that SIL had the right system of using local languages.

We received the other day a copy of *Tiempo* magazine of Mexico. It contained a full-page article about the UNESCO literacy award given for our work in Papua New Guinea. After telling, in a way that is convincing to those who read it, that we are doing a wonderful work—a work that needs to be done, a work that is appreciated—the article closed by saying that we are undergoing attacks, especially in Colombia, Ecuador, and Mexico, and that some of these attacks come from religious groups. Some attacks come from people who want the Indians to continue in their old customs, their old witchcraft, their old revenge killings, all those exotic activities which journalists love to write about. Some are distressed because when we give Indians the Bible they give up some of those things which handicap them in their own nation and become citizens of Mexico, of Peru—full-fledged citizens, like Manuel Arenas.

"I am an Indian."

Did you ever hear Manuel speak? He was one of the Indians of Mexico who was reached through a Bible translator, Herman Aschmann. He did not lose his love for his people. At one of the places where he spoke he began his message by saying "I am an Indian." He was proud of it. But he spoke five languages and could thrill people as he presented the gospel to them. One of the Christians of Turkey is a doctor who was led to the Lord by Manuel and a Spanish doctor. The two of them brought this man to Christ.

The third group which this article identified as trying to undermine our work are people who mistakenly believe we are political. But God can raise up defenders for us. In this international magazine published in Mexico City we are being defended.

When you are under attack and being criticized, lied about, and opposed, and when people are trying to stop you from doing the task to which God has called you, you need to have your soul flooded with God's love.

On our first trip to the USSR we became acquainted with one of the two outstanding linguists of the world and his wife. We were invited to the home of a linguist who cooperated with him—a lady whose husband showed interest in the Bible. I brought out a copy. The two men showed enough interest to read it right there at the table, first listening to a portion I read, and then looking at it themselves. The principal linguist even got close to the light so he could see better to read the Bible. The woman linguist made fun of him. But today she seems to be a believer in the Lord Jesus Christ because, when her husband died, she experienced the need for God's love in her heart. The Word of God became precious to her and she accepted the gift of a Bible.

About four years ago the distinguished professor and his wife asked permission to leave the USSR. Permission was given. Now he is a professor of linguistics at Yale University. We visited them when we came back from the USSR the first part of November; things worked out beautifully for them. Elaine showered love upon this lady, who was lonely and disturbed. They had bought a big house; nobody else lived there. Her kids were all in various universities, studying. She wanted to know how to use the typewriter, so Elaine gave her pointers and then sent her a book. Recently we received a perfectly typed letter that she had written.

The letter has a ring to it which shows that God is working in her life. It results from the love that we showed them in Moscow and then had opportunity to show again in this country.

We have a commission to fulfill. That commission is to take His message of love to all who have never heard.

We Are Neighbors!

Ronald Gluck

It was not quite what I had expected from my lunch guest. After greeting me and my two colleagues, the ambassador of an African country to the United Nations went straight to the point. "This is a very busy time because the General Assembly just reconvened September 15. I should be with my foreign minister who is visiting, but I told my secretary to be sure to allow room for you in my schedule. It did not work out for us to meet two years ago when you were in New York, and I did not want to miss this opportunity again."

I apologized for not seeing him in 1990, but he did not seem to hear.

"Before being posted to this position I was the prefect for six years in a prefecture where some of your people were working. I saw how simply they lived, how they helped my people to write their language, and how they taught farmers to read. On behalf of my country I want to thank you for what you are doing. It is wonderful what you are doing for my country. Please, the next time you are in New York I want you to come to my home and meet my wife and children."

All of this was said before we had even looked at the menu!

He continued, "I live only several hundred meters from your branch center in my city, the capital. We are neighbors." There was little I could say, but I thanked him and assured him I would pass on his comments to the SIL director in his country. When I added that a goal of our linguists is also to see that the New Testament is translated into the local languages, he smiled and said, "I know."

I mentioned that, in light of the pictures of ethnocide and starving Somalis appearing daily in the newspapers, I would like to offer a prayer of thanks to the Lord for the food in front of us. He agreed. I prayed, then handed him a listing of the forty-two languages spoken in his country. His finger went straight to Tem. "That's the language!" he exclaimed.

The SIL couple who kept this man informed of their activities in the Tem language for more than six years when he was the prefect did the rest of their branch members and themselves a great service.

While saying goodbye, he smiled broadly, commenting, "In my language my first two names mean 'God's destiny for me'. Each time I introduce myself I'm thanking God for my destiny." And then, climbing into the back of his limo, he invited us, at least twice more, to visit him at his home.

Long Labor - Fine Fruit

David Presson and Ronald Gluck

In 1986 the government of X had decided to construct an embassy building in Jerusalem. But since Islamic nations were unwilling to concede Jerusalem as the capital of Israel, bedlam broke out at the United Nations. "If you go ahead with your plans to put an embassy building in Jerusalem, my government will sever diplomatic ties with yours" was the message coming into Ambassador E's office from many others.

But E was not about to break his appointment with Ron Gluck and Aaron Hoffman. Welcoming them in the midst of the melee, he continued to bark orders to aides and to keep traffic moving. Six-foot-long telexes from his president draped his desk. Aides kept scampering in and out of his office. The phone rang. His country's ambassador to Cairo was on the line. He was being called to the Foreign Ministry of Egypt. "What should I tell him?" the ambassador asked.

Ron knew E well enough by now to ask a loaded question: "Are you Muslim or Christian?"

"Both," replied the ambassador without hesitation.

"May I pray for wisdom for you?" continued Ron, sensing that the visit should not be prolonged.

"Indeed!" agreed the harried ambassador, adding after Ron prayed, "Your prayer is the benediction to your visit."

Annually Ron continued his calls, always warmly welcomed by E. But as E's stature grew, he became his country's Minister of Foreign Affairs and could not spend as much time in New York. Ron's loss, however, was gain for SIL in the country of X. When branch director John Maire and his associate David Presson believed it was time to seek an agreement with their host nation's Ministry of Foreign Affairs, David and John found Ron's friend, the minister, well disposed. The process took time, because other ministries had to be consulted and give consent.

But in March 1995, David was able to deliver to E's cabinet director a copy of an article written by the minister and published in the USA. "Do you know the minister?" asked the cabinet director.

David answered, "Not I personally, but I have a friend in Washington, DC, who knows His Excellency."

The cabinet director was more than pleased to be able to help speed the process along. A month later the agreement, ensuring SIL visas, residence cards, and tax-free importation privileges, was signed by E and Randy Groff, SIL director at that time.

"Whatever happened to the plan to build an embassy in Jerusalem?" someone asked.

"The building went up," came the reply. "It is occupied, and no diplomatic relations were severed."

E.

Avoid cutting corners.

A Klutz among the Elite

Lester Troyer

The office of Secretary of the President's Cabinet in the Philippines is the ranking office in the cabinet and one of the most powerful offices of the administration. The Lord, through an interesting set of circumstances, gave us a very close and unique friendship with the Secretary of the Cabinet of one of the administrations while I was director of the branch during the late '60s.

This man had a true interest in the ethnic minorities' economic plight as well as a scholarly one in their diverse and fascinating cultures. He not only visited our center at Nasuli in the south but also flew out to several tribal locations where our SIL people were working. My staff and I took him some of the materials we had worked on in the languages and ethnology of some of the groups. These he read avidly, with interest and appreciation.

Our ties became so close that he repeatedly called me in for consultation on various matters related to the minorities. One morning I received a call from Malacanang Palace asking me to prepare myself right away. The secretary was leaving on a motorcade south through the province beyond Manila. I quickly complied and arrived at the palace in time to be escorted by one of the secret service people to the secretary's limousine. With motorcycle escort and a bevy of security and press people behind us in the entourage, we sliced through Manila traffic in a manner to which I was unaccustomed!

The secretary had other expatriate experts with him. He was on a tour looking over the farming conditions in the particular province and was eager to get various leaders from differing disciplines to interact. The other two men were also Caucasian Westerners. They were able to cite and recite all kinds of statistics from their fields of interest. I was interested and had been talking with the secretary previously of the needs for community development among the ethnic minorities and of the ways our programs would lead into that phase of service, given the right designing of our and the government's resources.

But alas—I had never taken time to get briefed on the statistics we needed to make our conversations fruitful. Now I felt tongue-tied. I fear I came across to the well-informed men as a bit of a klutz. I may have been a disappointment to my friend, the secretary. But I learned a lesson. Be well-informed before you pull out the soap box and begin "beating the drums" for action. This is especially important if you form a close liaison with high officials who are bright and have the good of their country and people at heart.

A Close Call

Extract from a 1990 letter to Richard Pittman.

A number of years ago there was a lack of communication between the provincial police office and the district office which ended up causing me to inadvertently offend the district police officials. I had been told I did not need to report my presence in the area to the district police, as long as I reported to the police post nearest to my village. I did this and ended up getting a very stern letter from the district police station, demanding that I come immediately to their office to report. The problem was that it was a three-day walk or two-day motorboat trip to reach their office. Fortunately, our airstrip was due to be officially checked out in a few days, so I arranged to have the checkout aircraft fly me to the district center for some time on the ground to mend fences.

When I arrived at the district police office, I was met by an officer who was icily cold in his interactions with me. I waited before his desk while he shuffled papers for about half an hour. When he finally decided to talk with me, he tore into me for:

(1) failing to report to his office upon arrival in the area and (2) failing to keep him fully informed on the progress of the airstrip at our home village. (The latter is another case where we followed all the rules of reporting but did no more.) I tried to explain that I had followed all the rules in both cases and had been told that I did not need to inform other parties personally.

Finally this officer (now a good friend) said, "No need? No need! You are a Christian and the Bible instructs you to honor the government God has established on this earth! What's more, you probably have not even let the civilian official know what you are doing out there!" He decided to call the civilian district officer to check out his hunch. Fortunately, that officer had been kept fully informed and strongly came to our aid, supporting our work and affirming his agreement with our constructing the airstrip.

This seemed to help ease the tension in the interview. I finally left with several lessons in mind: (1) Always report to more people than you have to. It cannot hurt, and it may end up helping a lot. (2) Just interacting with civilian officials is not enough. (3) Reporting is a way of showing respect, as well as a means of assuring information flow. (4) Having reported to someone faithfully, and through that having made a friend, was the key factor in my being forgiven the offense I had caused.

The High Cost of Short Circuits

Jose Estrella

When I was in charge of visa applications and importation paper work for a branch of SIL, a member fouled his visa up in such a way that under normal procedure it would have taken at least a month and a half to remedy it. On top of that, he wanted to leave the country the next day. My advice was simple, and had he followed it, things would have been all right. He did not want to go that route, so he took the matter to the director and to my immediate boss. They sided with the member and asked me to short-circuit the ordinary route.

Since the private secretary of the man in charge of the Immigration Office was a good friend of mine, I went to him for help. He immediately assigned his own secretary to help me straighten out the problem. This man took me to five heads of departments and in a matter of two hours everything was taken care of. But at what a cost!

For two months I was no longer accepted as a friend by the fine men who were bypassed by the shortcut. In fact, I completely lost the friendship of one of them. I had overstepped their authority in an area where outside pressure, especially from their top man's office, was not welcome. I had humiliated them, making them drop everything they were doing and pull some of their secretaries out to take care of "my" request. They had to stop their clock and give me their undivided attention. It hurt them especially when they saw their "friend" standing with the man who was ordering them to straighten out the visa.

Seat of the Scornful

Richard Pittman

Some years ago I was invited to a doctrinal examination of a candidate who had studied at a large ecclesiastical university in one of the countries where we work. The examiners were all clergymen with high-ranking degrees in their fields. They were from a non-American nation and the examination was being conducted in a language other than English. I do not know whether the examiners realized that I understood the language. I suspect that, in any case, they did not care.

The student being examined had done much research in American sources for his thesis and was apparently quoting some of these sources approvingly. The clergy, however, did not share his enthusiasm for the people he quoted and poured contempt on the authorities he cited.

"Do you know what we do when an American stands up to speak in our country?" asked one of the examiners. "We all laugh!"

The scorn in the question and in its answer was withering.

If the intent of the examiners was to embarrass me, the only American present, their purpose was mercifully frustrated. I felt very much at ease and was not troubled in the slightest. I knew that not only many Americans, including myself, are capable of saying foolish things, but also many nationals of other countries. Fortunately, I did not feel the slightest bit defensive.

The experience served a very useful purpose, however. I was reminded again how extremely important it is that we in SIL never allow ourselves to sit in the seat of the scornful as these examiners were doing. Whether or not the young man on the hot seat deserved the scathing remarks being made about his work, SIL members should not indulge in the luxury of making such remarks to or about anyone. In confrontations with even our most hostile critics, we should be vividly reminded of Michael, the archangel, who, when contending with the devil about the body of Moses, "durst not bring against him a railing accusation, but said, The Lord rebuke thee."

On one of my trips through India, since I was going to a cold country, I carried a warm topcoat. But the India segment of the trip was blistering hot. The passengers on the plane I was in were allowed, therefore, to keep cool in the airport lounge during a refueling stop.

"Did some passenger lose this scarf?" called a stewardess, walking through the lounge and waving an attractive woolen muffler.

What stupid traveler would carry a warm scarf in a hot place like this? I scornfully mused.

Hours later, too late to claim it, I realized that I was the stupid owner of the lost scarf!

"So I would not sit in the scorner's seat nor hurl the cynic's ban. Let me live in a house by the side of the road and be a friend of man."

To Write or Not to Write

Richard Pittman

The cult of "honesty" (tell all) makes us feel it important not only to write negative feelings toward certain people but also to record our irritation with the country we live in, interviews we have had, and people with whom we rub elbows.

There may be some therapeutic or safety-valve value in doing this at certain times or places, especially in "speaking the truth in love," face-to-face and alone, to one with whom we disagree. In fact, there are strong exhortations in the Bible to do just that. (Matthew 5:23,24; 18:15) But committing the criticism to writing, either to the adversary or about an adversary you identify, is something else. In most cases it should not be done.

On my first visit to the Philippines I was given a very useful list of languages of the Philippines which included, along with language data, a critical comment about a veteran missionary. The writer, of course, never intended that the missionary should see the comment. And I forgot all about the comment until, as I was visiting the missionary and mentioned the list, he asked if he might see it. I produced it, handed it over, then watched in shock as he winced at the criticism written against him. I later learned that the criticism was only hearsay and had very little basis in fact. I came to admire the veteran very much. How I wished I had never shown him the language list, and how the writer of the comment wished the comment had never been written!

Early in the days of the Peace Corps, a Peace Corps worker in Africa wrote a postcard home with some uncomplimentary remarks about the country in which she was working. The card was read by postal employees in the host country, shown to higher authorities, and created such a disturbance as to greatly harm and hinder the Peace Corps work in that place.

So how can a person communicate his concerns, misgivings, and warnings? In cases where it is a host country or citizens of the host country who are likely to be mentioned, do not do it in writing. In most cases, in fact, it is better not to verbalize criticisms at all.

"A bird," warned Solomon, "will carry the voice, and that which hath wings will tell the matter." (Ecclesiastes 10:20)

That Wycliffe Bible Bunch!
Barbara Shannon

One day Al had to visit a bishop who lives just a block from our house. (We have since forgotten, because of the event that followed, just what his errand was that day.) As he approached the bishop's open office door, he heard an angry voice shatter the morning stillness in the monastery. "That Wycliffe Bible bunch! Something ought to be done about them! They're a menace to this country and ought to be expelled."

Quickly retreating to the farthest corner of the waiting room, Al stood wondering what to do. Presently an angry man came storming out of the bishop's office and, with a gruff "*Buenos dias,*" went on by and out the door. During Al's interview with the bishop which immediately followed, the Catholic clergyman encouraged him to "build some bridges" with the man who had just been there, giving him his name and address.

We began by visiting him in his office. After having him to our house for a meal, we discovered that he was a wonderful person. We soon grew to love him—with God's love and with our own love, too. The upset had been a misunderstanding and was quickly put to rights. He came to supper one night with two other bishops; since all three were in charge of different Indian groups in the Peruvian jungle, we presented them with just-translated New Testaments for those languages. They accepted them with deep feeling and appreciation.

Soon afterward, when five New Testaments, each in a different language, were presented at a ceremony in Lima, the cardinal of Peru was asked to come and speak. He personally apologized to us for not being able to make it but said he would send one of his bishops to be his representative. The man who came had the following to say:

"I believe there is no work more effective, more important and transcendent, than to be a messenger of the Word of God. I sincerely believe that one of the most hopeful and consoling signs of our times is the diffusion of the Word of God. The Word of God transforms completely when we listen to it with faith, humility, and love."

He said many more fine words about our translators, about Uncle Cam, and our group as a whole—using no notes and speaking with a depth of emotion which is impossible to capture on paper. Our director also spoke, as did a very fine evangelical Peruvian in the government. The Minister of Education gave a wonderful speech, and five Indian men read Scriptures, each in his own tongue.

But what thrilled me most was what the cardinal's representative had to say about God's Word and the work of Wycliffe. He was *that same man* who had stormed out of our friend's office just a few months before!

Loaded Words

Richard Pittman

It comes as a surprise to most persons of European extraction to discover that many of the words he uses without a second thought are loaded when used in Asia.

People in that part of the world, for example, dislike intensely to be referred to as Asiatics or Orientals. But it is quite all right to refer to them as Asians.

When they are seeking to attract tourists, they, of course, use words like *Orient* or *Far East*, which sound exotic to tourists. But they do not appreciate the inference that the center of the earth is Europe or America as is implied by terms like *Orient* or *Far East*. They would prefer Asia, or specific country names.

Filipinos feel that referring to their country as the Philippine Islands makes it sound small or weak or fractured. They much prefer to call it "The Philippines." Filipino is also often spelled "Pilipino," but *never* "Philipino."

Officials of most countries dislike very much to hear a couple of foreigners refer to a language group as "our tribe" and its language as "our language." The word *tribe* itself is considered derogatory in some countries. "Cultural minority," "minority language group," or "cultural community" are usually better.

Certain religious terms are not appreciated in many countries of Asia. The designation "missionary" is especially disliked in many countries. Indirect reference to "other missionaries" may, by implication, classify a person with them.

The first person plural pronoun should not be used in reports. It often gives the impression of "first plural exclusive." That is, "This is the project of us foreigners but not of you nationals who read this report."

Even criticism of unspecified parties referred to only as "they," "them," or "it" can be interpreted as criticisms of the country and/or people of the country in which the criticism is heard.

The word *informant* is especially wrong to use. For many people it is understood to mean *informer* or *quisling*.

The word *survey* is frightening to many because it raises the specter of spying.

Many words have a military sound: *base, advance, occupy, strategy.* However dynamic they may seem when used in home circles, they should not be used in host countries.

Any allusions or inferences which may seem to imply connections with intelligence agencies should be scrupulously avoided. Excessive interest in maps and map terminology can be suspect.

A "professional" interest in, or use of, political topics and terminology can make a person seem to be a government representative rather than a linguist. On the other hand, a person *should* be a professional in his ability to use linguistic and educational terms.

All terms which can be interpreted as racist should be avoided.

Shall We Blast Our Hosts?

Richard Pittman

By the time Magsaysay had been president of the Philippines for a year, he had taken at least three initiatives which troubled me. He planned to reintroduce bullfights, a national lottery, and diplomatic relations with the Vatican, none of which had characterized the Philippines since the days when the country was a colony of Spain.

Fired up with fervor, I sat down and wrote him a letter, quoting Scripture.

That was certainly better than "going public" with an article denouncing him. But I erred badly by sending it to him through the mail. I should have carried it to him personally and given him a chance to object personally. He never refused our requests for an audience.

In spite of my foolishness in mailing instead of hand-carrying my letter of concern, the president wrote a very courteous acknowledgment. Then, to my astonishment, I observed that the plans for bullfights and a national lottery were quietly scrapped, and the ambassador to Italy was given responsibility for diplomatic relations with the Vatican. Best of all, communication with the president was not interrupted. We were allowed to continue working in the country and calling on him just as before.

Not long after this incident, our translators with one of the Manobo groups reported that lowland settlers were taking land away from the Manobos. After attempting to make sure we had our facts straight, I took the matter up personally with the president the next time I saw him. "Get Congressman X (who represented that area) on the phone," said the president to an aide. An attempt was made on the spot. The call was not completed while we were in the office, but knowing Magsaysay's promptness in dealing with matters, I have no doubt it went through later. There was at least temporary relief for the Manobos in that location.

After Magsaysay's untimely death we needed to complete arrangements for starting the work of JAARS in the Philippines. The president had told us how to do it, but we were not yet off the ground at the time he lost his life in an airplane accident. So we took the matter to his Minister of Defense, through whom we had been told to work. "Just consider that Magsaysay has never died," the minister advised us. It was his way of saying that the late president's instructions would be carried out as though he were still alive. And they were.

The Apostle Paul had to work under Emperor Nero, whose name is synonymous with greater repression than any of us has known. Given Paul's eloquence with the pen, it is significant that he neither launched a personal protest against Nero's oppression nor incited any of his colleagues or assistants to do so. On the contrary, he wrote to the believers in Rome (of all places!): "Everyone must obey state authorities, because no authority exists without God's permission, and the existing authorities have been put there by God. Whoever opposes the existing authorities opposes what God has ordered; and anyone who does so will bring judgment on himself."

On one occasion in the Philippines there was a flurry of activity honoring Mary, which some interpreted as idolatry. I was both incensed and frustrated because I could not think how to fight it. Recalling Uncle Cam's advice, "The best way to fight the machine is to love the individual," I remembered an influential priest to whom I had promised some linguistic material. I took the material and called on him. I could tell from the course of our conversation that the Lord was working in his heart as well as in mine. I came away reassured that, in spite of my imaginings, God was doing things to right wrongs.

A (Not So) Soft Answer

Jose Estrella

There was a time in one country when it seemed that our visa problems were over. Everyone started getting visa approvals. Then, suddenly and inexplicably, several visas were denied.

We visited the head of the department to find out the reason. In the conversation, he made it clear that several years before, when he was visiting a town in the jungle, he saw one of our planes land on the town's airstrip. He went over to look at the airplane. As he stood looking at it, he heard the pilot scream at him, "Get out of here! You have no right to be near the airplane!"

Is it any wonder that as soon as he came into power he tried to stop our work?

He Rose to the Bait

Richard Pittman

Two favorite types of baiting catch expatriates. The first takes place overseas. A malcontent comes seeking help. The foreigner came to give help. So he rises to the occasion, lending a sympathetic ("therapeutic," he believes) ear. But the recital of the sufferer's woes gradually turns to blame of the powers-that-be. What began as a kindly listening to a friend in need ends with, "Yes, yes. I understand. It's too bad. There ought to be a law against it." And the conversation becomes not a confession of the speaker's sins but a claim of government wrongs.

The second type takes place when the expatriate returns home. He is now a hero. His admiring audience hangs on his words. In the question session they commiserate with him over his sufferings—unhygienic conditions, primitive people, demonic powers, unbelievably bad governments. And the words of the incautious traveler get back to the government of the land where he was a guest.

Most insidious of all is the temptation to betray your host. It is never suggested, of course, as a form of betrayal. The opening gambit is that you are an "authority" by virtue of your firsthand experiences in a foreign land. And it is suggested that providing information to your interrogator will "protect" your host from the sinister forces which would destroy him. But if the interrogator is an intelligence agent, you may very well become a potential or actual traitor to the people you came to serve.

A retired American colonel was on his way to visit the CIA one day and was tempted to take an SIL member with him. But then he decided against it because, as he explained to the SILer later, "If you give them (the CIA) intelligence information, you are a spy."

On another occasion, a friendly U.S. university official sent a CIA official to see the director of an SIL session at that university, "just in case the director might have some information of interest for him." The director courteously explained he was trusted by the national officials of the country in which he worked and to give information on that country would be to betray that trust. He also explained that the results of the SIL linguistic studies would be published for all to see and use. The CIA official accepted this polite refusal and did not press further for information.

But how can you know whether it is an intelligence agent questioning you? The best answer to that is to refuse permission to any SIL member to give political or military intelligence about any country, or any other type of information which could be used to endanger the security of a country. Each SILer should be obliged to maintain a firm position of not being qualified to report on political, military, or intelligence matters.

A good many people who have been raised in "free speech" countries regard freedom of speech not only as a sacred right but even as an obligation. SIL members, however, have exactly the opposite obligation in their role as expatriate guests in countries not their own. The "privilege" of talking like an authority against countries they have visited or lived in as expatriates is not theirs.

Does this sound too negative? Does it leave them nothing to say? Not at all. There are good bits of information about the people and culture of every country in the world which can be freely shared. If, in fact, the SILer loves people in the countries he goes to as he claims, he should make known to others the admirable qualities of the people he has seen.

You Would Have Thought He Was for Real

Jose Estrella

One morning a clean-cut individual dressed like a clergyman showed up in my office. He told me that from childhood he had had a tremendous desire to serve God, especially among the Indians. He had heard about SIL and wanted to find how he could work with us. His evangelical language was perfect. You would have thought he had grown up in a Christian environment and that his only desire was to serve Christ and the Indians.

What beautiful language he spoke! It was too bad he could not be of any help. I told him that I was very much impressed by his heart's desire. I told him I would put him in contact with a Roman Catholic priest who does religious work in the area he mentioned. Since he claimed to want to convert Indians, I told him that we as a linguistic organization were not allowed to do religious proselyting.

My answer caught him off guard. For the next hour he tried to engage me in a conversation which was purely religious. He even said that since we were in such need of good press, he had friends who could help us.

It was during this time that he slipped and gave himself away. He belonged to a magazine which had started a campaign to kick SIL out of the country. Much of it was dedicated to publishing negative reports about us.

He Was Baiting Me

Richard Pittman

I was trying to sell our program in a country with a far-right political persuasion. The man assigned to interview me got onto politics. "How can we let you come in," he complained, "when we have our hands so full of problems caused by our enemies on the far left?"

"Our program will help you defeat those enemies," I confidently assured him, going on to explain how the literacy, dignity, and loyalty we would generate could turn the tide in their war for men's minds.

The only trouble was that my interrogator was probably not representing the side I thought he was at all. He was almost certainly baiting me—setting a trap to use against me when the time was ripe. All that I said about literacy, dignity, and liberty was good, but the minute I attached a political label to it I was out of bounds.

The Lord rebuked me immediately. And He has continued to remind me that we must not be anti-any political party, religious label, or denominational group. We are indeed to be anti-hatred, but no one group has exclusive addiction to hatred. Nor does any one group have an exclusive claim on goodness. Our good contributions need to be explained and our stand against wrong included—but not on a platform pro or con any guilt-by-label individual or group.

Penny-wise, Franc-foolish

Ronald Gluck

Sometime in 1975 or 1976, during the *hamattan* season, I had the privilege of flying two officials of the Department of Civil Aviation to Bamenda, Cameroon, to inspect a new strip that a certain mission wished to open. These gentlemen came at the request of the mission. It was to be an overnight trip.

On our arrival at Bamenda, the missionary there informed the two officials and me that I was invited to stay overnight at the mission at their expense but that the others must go to a hotel in town. They followed those instructions, and I accepted the missionary's invitation.

At the time I was very grateful for the missionary's kindness, but in retrospect I have wished that I had refused his hospitality and spent a few extra francs to pass the night with my two friends.

Why? (1) By accepting the missionary's invitation I identified myself with him as another missionary and negated our nonsectarian status. (2) By turning my back on my friends within the Department of Civil Aviation, under whom I was responsible in matters relating to aviation, I lost a priceless opportunity to develop their friendship.

My decision was wrong in every aspect, one which I have regretted ever since.

La Prensa or *El Comercio*?

Douglas Deming

Flying the Amazon jungle circuit, I soon learned the wisdom of Uncle Cam's advice to take current newspapers or magazines to lonely priests, nuns, soldiers, plantation owners in isolated wilderness outposts. If I ran out of journals I would even give autographed pictures of myself, often to discover, years later, that they were prominently displayed in some place of honor, perhaps near the "saints"!

On one flight with many stops I ran out of fresh news resources before I had to land at a distant military post. "Any news?" asked the local commander, who had come down many steps to meet me at the dock. He was hoping for a new newspaper.

"*Ay, mi comandante*," I groaned. "What can I say? I have arrived empty-handed."

"Captain," he replied, only half in jest, "you belong to the Institute which teaches people to read and write, but you bring me nothing on which to practice my reading skills!" My chagrin was exceeded only by his disappointment.

But the lesson was not lost. Some time later I had occasion to land at a jungle strip manned by an unfriendly officer. We were greeted, in fact, by soldiers in trenches near the airstrip, with weapons trained on us. I smelled Trouble with a capital *T* as the scowling commander walked menacingly toward the plane.

Putting on my most engaging smile, I greeted him as he reached the plane. *"Buenos dias, mi comandante,"* I said ingratiatingly, extending two different newspapers. "Which would you prefer, *La Prensa* or *El Comercio?*"

"I will take both," he replied curtly.

With relief I noticed the soldiers in the trenches had lowered their carbines and were beginning to walk away, at ease.

Camaraderie

Douglas Deming

There is audible celestial talk! I have heard it. I have even been in on the exchange.

A word can trigger a long thought process, a cascade of memories...or conviction!

The last Peruvian flight I piloted was over the four-mile-high spikes of the Andean Mountains, a flight fringing celestial realms and filled with the beauty between distant horizons. It involved conversation with other pilots and with air traffic controllers.

Reporting position, time, and altitude to Pucallpa radio I heard, *"Roe-hair, Linguistico doce noventaiuno; y don Day-meeng Doo-glaas, no nos olvides.* (Roger, Linguistics 1291; and Mr. Douglas Deming, don't forget us.) Return soon!"

Memories! Many hot, muggy hours in the jungle radio shack with my air traffic controller friends...

Another voice—almost a whisper—over the VHF radio, *"Doo-glaas?"*

"Si."

From the cockpit of a far-off DC-8, *"Tu vas a regresar?"* (You will return?)

"Si, Jorge, tal vez." (Yes, perhaps...)

Silent thoughts...

The many nights Jorge has been in our home. Meals...conversing at the table. The move to more comfortable seating, and conversation to the cacophony of insects and mosquitoes pestering the living room screens. What does Jorge think of Jesus?

Silent prayer…

Another airliner. Another former student. *"Ola, Dooog."* I recognized the deep, resonant voice.

"Ola, Carlos. Que tal?"

His voice continued, *"Hay tiempo*—you have time for a *cafecito* in Lima, no?"

How my children adored Carlos! A TV star. Personable, elegant—and from one of the top-named families of the Lima society. They pray for Carlos too!

But back down to earth. Breaking over the backbone of the Andes it is a long way down—down to Lima. "Line of sight" provides direct radio contact with Lima Control. An instrument approach. Clipped instructions. Clipped responses. You listen to the control of each airplane, imagining their respective position…viewing…knowing their unseen maneuvers for Lima's misty runway on the shore of the pounding Pacific Ocean.

"Cap-ee-tan Dooglaas?" The deep, clear voice of approach control.

"Si."

"Le habla Juan (John talking). When are you leaving for the U.S.?"

"Buenos dias, Juan. Manana—at 14:55 zulu." I responded, using my best captain's voice.

"Caramba! I have duty at this position! After you check in for your flight tomorrow, please come up to the cab. Cleared for the ILS runway 15 approach. Report passing Ventanilla. I want to see you before you go."

Because of a several-hour preboarding hassle on our international flight and the additional frustrations of each passenger's identifying his luggage for additional inspection before boarding the airliner, Sue and I were tired. We finally relaxed in our assigned seats.

"*Cap-ee-tan Day-meeng?*" The voice of the stewardess emanated from speakers over each seat of the Boeing 707.

My raised hand indicated my position.

Juan hurriedly left the side of the stewardess for my seat. The *abrazo*—the Latin hug of greeting. I had forgotten to visit him! He had left his work to come say goodbye.

How could I have forgotten? One hot afternoon eight years before, in the jungle, Juan accepted the Messiah in our living room.

They Never Give Me a Report

Richard Pittman

I was reading a critical newspaper article. The target of the criticism was SIL, so my reaction was mixed—rejecting much of what I read because I knew it to be untrue but watching warily for a shoe which might fit and therefore have to be put on.

Suddenly I caught a fatal phrase. The reporter quoted a high government official as saying, "I do not know what SIL does. They never give me a report."

I had no idea whether the reporter and/or official was telling the truth or not. But I did know that if this detail were true, someone in SIL had been remiss. A written report, at least once a year, designed to be read by all of the officials who are most responsible for us, is a must for every country in which SIL works.

Lest this seem too much to ask, I would hasten to add that there is no reason why it should be an expensive, illustrated, book-like production. A neat mimeographed piece without pictures is entirely adequate. In fact, there are some serious considerations for not using pictures. Pictures of expatriates can give a wrong or undesirable impression. Certainly they invite comparisons which can easily be invidious.

There is also a temptation to substitute an expensive annual report for serious publication of carefully done linguistic books and articles. This should be resisted. Fine linguistic production is our best credential, not an elaborate report of our work.

Should the report include a listing of hymnbooks and Scripture publications printed during the year in question? No. For several reasons:

1. Every government, whether secular or church-related, is responsible to its citizens to be evenhanded in dealing with competing religious systems, including those which reject religion. The translation of documents which are perceived as religious, therefore, is a highly sensitive issue, especially when it is done by expatriates. Admittedly some countries have allowed such translation to be specifically identified in contracts which they have signed, but if we then say, "The government contracted for us to translate New Testaments," we put the government in a difficult position. In the strictest sense they did not contract for us to translate New Testaments. They contracted for us to do technical, nonreligious work which could benefit their citizens of all persuasions. The translation was permitted because of our urging.

2. Inclusion of "religious" material in an annual report invites possibly awkward comparison with linguistic and literacy material published during the same time.

3. The importance of being accountable for man hours spent in the host country may seem to be satisfied by a large volume of translation published, and this may salve the conscience for not doing "practical" projects. But every host country wants to see a substantial output of project effort which all citizens recognize as being of "practical" benefit to the country. Unless a branch is struggling to keep up its output of such contributions, it may lose its acceptability with its host.

Does that mean the translation should be hidden? No. The beautiful, effective way to report it is by inviting officials to the dedications of New Testaments, presenting copies to high officials in personal visits, telling stirring stories of the effects of the translations on those who have read them. Uncle Cam presented a copy of his Cakchiquel New Testament years ago to the president of Guatemala. When a Cakchiquel came to the president protesting something or someone, the president produced the New Testament and urged him to read it. He could not have done so if all he had was a report which told of the translation.

Should the annual report to a host government include a financial statement? The problem is that SIL members are volunteers, responsible for their own support. The organization is not in a position, therefore, to give a complete financial report for all its members to a host government. If the host government or a funding agency expects a financial report of a specific project, that should be done in the way expected in a report devoted to that project.

How about the long lists of names of expatriates? Some government offices (e.g., immigration) may routinely request or expect such lists. Others may be annoyed by them. It seems wise in such cases to prepare lists as addenda or supplements to the annual report and present them only to those offices which need to be kept informed.

Is there a way to reconcile the need to give glory to those with whom we work, while admitting our responsibility for the work we are doing? Definitely. When highly commendable successes have been achieved, names of nationals, individuals in cultural minorities, should be given maximum credit if at all possible. Names of expatriates should be featured much less, except where ultimate responsibility must be assigned. Far more authorship credit should be given to tribal authors for work on dictionary and folklore materials than has been done in the past.

Can written reports be a substitute for personal visits? Not really. Even a written report should be hand-carried, if at all possible, to each official for whom a copy is intended, and a friendly conversation should be developed around it. What better excuse for calling on the one who said, "They never give me a report."

II

SECOND CONCERN: THEIR LANGUAGE

As a scientific linguistic organization, we have the purpose and privilege of doing language analysis, creating an alphabet, translating parts of the Bible, and promoting literacy in previously unwritten languages.

———————

———————

Cameron Townsend:

You have to be a good scientist in the field of descriptive linguistics in order to do a good translation. A reader must not find a swatch of grammatical errors and wonder why God cannot use good grammar!

———————

You may have to work for ten or fifteen years, but you are going to produce something that will not return fruitless unto God, but will go on bearing fruit for years and years.

———————

We pioneer because we feel that every tribe must hear the message of salvation... We need to go to people and tell them in their own language the story which means so much to us—that of God's love.

A.

Help them meet their language and literacy goals.

Vernacular Languages

Kenneth Pike

One reason it is so important to use the mother tongue for literacy work and Bible translation instead of teaching the official language is that much of a person's identity is rooted in his language. He feels himself to be what he is, based on what his language is. If you force him to drop his vernacular language, you force him to change his identity structure as he sees himself.

If you want him to think of himself with self-respect, you must encourage him to keep using his language as long as he wants to, until he is motivated to learn the national language for other reasons. It is important for his self-identity, for his survival, to be able to have his own language.

Language and Man's Dignity

Article translated from Spanish, originally published in Gente, Lima, March 17, 1978, by Dr. Miro Quesada, an outstanding scholar and philosopher who has served his native Peru as Minister of Education and in many other capacities.

A few days ago the third convention of the Summer Institute of Linguistics in Latin America took place in Lima. As is common knowledge, this institution, motivated by a desire to spread the Christian faith in areas remote from what we, perhaps euphemistically, call the "centers of civilization," has carried on scientific and pedagogical studies of high quality. In order to translate the Bible into all languages, especially those which are spoken by isolated groups which have neither alphabet, grammar, nor dictionary, they have made thorough studies of very highest scientific quality of various languages. These studies have cost them years of work and sacrifice, since the only way to carry these out is to live in places where the languages are spoken.

Scientific results of labor

The results of their labors have been very fine indeed. Today the scientific world can point to grammars, dictionaries, and reading-and-writing manuals for an enormous number of languages—languages which, until recently, we proud and domineering Westerners considered primitive. Besides having accomplished this enormous amount of scientific work, the people of SIL have also helped the various groups whose languages they have studied to evaluate and learn numerous skills tailored to their area. These skills increase food production, facilitate house construction, and improve the standard of living of the people.

Although they have done this, they have at the same time been careful to respect the customs and ways of life of these original inhabitants of our continent. In order to impart the aforementioned skills, they have chosen the most intelligent men and women of each group and have encouraged them to be teachers of their own people. In this way they have succeeded in communicating the most needed fundamentals within the framework of the native cultures, without forcing alien thought patterns on them and without the imposition of humiliating attitudes and values from the outside world.

Respect for native culture

We must recognize that there is indeed in the teachings of Christ great innovation. But Christianity, with very few exceptions (cannibalism and polygamy are two of them), is compatible with the customs and lifestyles of any people. It is much more compatible, we would say, than any of the philosophies created by the West, such as existentialism or Marxism. The Summer Institute of Linguistics has accomplished the feat of Christianizing numerous groups which have been isolated from "civilization," influencing in a minimal way their lifestyle, their folklore, and their basic cultural orientation. How have they been able to accomplish this? It is hard to say. But there is no doubt that one of the factors which has contributed most to giving SIL people this profound capacity for spiritual influence combined with respect for the native culture is their being highly qualified linguists. In addition, they have dedicated the better part of their lives to studying the so-called "primitive" languages. Naturally, they have discovered something which they already knew—that there is no such thing as a "primitive" language. But it is one thing to know this because we have read it in some book or magazine, and it is quite another thing to experience personally the dazzling realization of proving this truth for one's self. This is just what they have done.

"His language is his dignity."

Kenneth Pike, president of the Institute, attended the convention. And in his words of appreciation for the friends of the Institute, he expressed in especially enlightening terms this highly distinctive quality of languages. Pike is a linguistic genius—creator of tagmemics, one of today's best known linguistic theories. Thanks to it, the technicians of SIL have been able to develop surprisingly effective techniques for grammatical analysis and translation. In disarmingly simple terms he made us see how any language, be it a group lost in the Amazon jungle or wandering over desert or tundra, is an astonishing creation, capable of expressing anything at all which those who use it need to say. Every language is rich in subtleties and unexpected possibilities. With delightful humor he showed how, in the languages which have for centuries been considered "primitive," there is a wealth of nuances, shades of meaning, and potential for expression, all of which demonstrate that there is not now, and never could have been, any essential difference between the intelligence of the originators of these languages and the intelligence of pedantic and conceited "Western man." "For this reason," affirmed Pike, "a person's first reading lessons should be taught him in his native tongue, because his language is at the very heart of his being and determines in a most essential way his personality. His language is his dignity."

It is this kind of respect, this unlimited admiration for the languages which they study and, consequently, for the people who speak them, which has undoubtedly enabled the people of the Summer Institute of Linguistics to teach their Indian hosts about Christ, respecting all the while their culture and way of life.

I Want My People to Have the Book of God

"Phil-in" July 1992

Thirty-five years ago when translator Dick Elkins was hiking through the lush green mountains of Mindanao, he came upon the remote village of Panganan nestled in a high valley. Two leaders of the local Matigsalug people greeted him and invited him to spend the night with them.

That evening Dick read to them from the Gospel of Mark which he had translated into a related dialect. When Dick closed the book, white-haired Chief Mangulibay took it and held it lovingly. Both leaders believed in Jesus as their Savior that night.

After three days of sharing the good news with the village, Dick was boarding a bamboo raft to leave when the chief said, "Come back soon; I want my people to have the book of God." Regretfully, Dick told them that because he was already working on a translation for another group, he could not help them.

But five years later, the chief's desire for God's Word still pulling at Dick's heart, he visited Panganan and showed the Matigsalug an ideal place for a grass airstrip which would be helpful if a translator were to come. He asked them not to plant crops or build houses there. They agreed and again asked him to come back.

Twenty-five years later Dick and his wife Betty, with Manobo translation assistants, finished translating the New Testament into Western Bukidnon Manobo. And, following the tugging of their hearts, they went to Panganan to translate God's Word for the Matigsalug people.

Hiking into Panganan, Dick wondered if the people had remembered his request about the airstrip. But how could they have managed to leave that strip of land unused for so long? It was too much to ask of farmers, with flat, plantable land so rare in that mountainous region.

As Dick reached the top of the last rise and looked down into the valley, he was amazed at what he saw: two long rows of houses running parallel and between them a wide stretch of uncultivated ground. It was the airstrip!

Today translation work continues among the Matigsalug.

Ethnocide...or Renaissance?

Richard Pittman

Years ago I was invited to speak at the University of Washington (Seattle) Anthropology Club. Though I have been a member of the American Anthropological Association for nearly forty years, I chose to identify myself initially as a Bible translator and began my talk like this:

"Regardless of the differences which you believe there are between anthropologists and Bible translators, there is at least one point on which we are totally united. Neither you nor we want to see the Indians of North and South America destroyed. Our reasons for wanting to see them live may be different, but all of you and all of us want them to live."

I then proceeded to report to them the well-documented case history of the Waorani (Aucas) being brought back from the verge of extinction by our Bible translators.

I did not at that time have as good documentation for the case of the Seri and Lacandon of Mexico, but both of these groups numbered fewer than 150 speakers when the Summer Institute of Linguistics began to study them. In the thirty-odd years that SIL has cooperated with the government in studying their languages, doing translation work, and helping them learn to read, both tribes have more than doubled their numbers. We are not claiming the glory; the Mexican government, in the case of the Seri and Lacandon, and the Ecuadorian government, in the case of the Aucas, worked hard to save these Indians from extinction. The story of the Chacobos in Bolivia is similar. The point is that SIL cooperation with governments is *not* a contribution to ethnocide, as some claim, but to indigenous renaissance in every finest sense of the word.

Greenland Eskimo

Let us take another example. Years ago a magazine, describing problems which afflicted a group of Canadian Eskimo, wondered wistfully why those Eskimo had not emerged into such remarkable virility as the Eskimo of Greenland, where, without losing their language and culture, they have produced lawyers, poets, and scholars. What the magazine failed to note was that distinguished Danish linguists translated the New Testament into Greenland Eskimo long ago, while the world failed to do the same for the specific group of Eskimo in focus in Canada.

With regard to the four or five thousand minority languages still spoken on the planet, there are two worlds of thought. One world would welcome the disappearance of the languages because they constitute barriers to communication and stumbling blocks to the education process. The other world would like to see them preserved because they are the central shrine of the culture, civilization, emotions, and thought of the people who speak them.

But it is possible to have the best of both worlds! As has been abundantly demonstrated, especially in Peru and the USSR, giving educational honor and recognition to minority languages as the initial medium of instruction makes subsequent teaching of the national language more rapid, enjoyable, and effective.

Will They Return
Our Women to Us?

Eugene Loos

In 1954 I took part in an expedition looking for the Mayoruna of Peru, a group whose language had never been studied. The trip lasted one month, deep in the jungle, but we never found them. Their history of attacking the Capanahua, among whom we had been working, was violent.

The Capanahua had suffered much at the hands of the Mayoruna, now called the Matses, who were killing the men in their attacks and carrying off women and children. They made slaves of the children and used the women to replace Matses girls who were killed at birth.

In 1969, when two SIL women, Harriet Fields and Hattie Kneeland, made peaceful contact with the Matses and were allowed to live with them, the Capanahua began to think that there might be a change. Indeed, the last raid occurred in 1971. One day in 1973 the chief of the Capanahua came to me and asked, "Brother, is it true that the Matses are allowing our SIL sisters to live among them?"

"Yes," I replied. "I am happy to report that they have accepted them and that the ladies are living there, learning the language."

"And can you tell me, Brother, will the Matses now return our women to us?" He was thinking of his niece, his cousin, his sisters. I felt as if I were between a sword and a wall.

"I do not know, Brother," I said to him. "I cannot do anything." Then I asked, "What do you think?"

He thought a while. Then he said, "Are the Matses also going to receive the Word of God in their language?"

"Yes," I told him, "in time."

"Then it is better that the women remain with them," he continued, "because I know that their husbands will not permit them to take their children with them; and if they leave without their children and find that their relatives here have died, that their homes have fallen down, and that their garden plots have grown up in weeds, they are not going to be happy here either. It is better that they stay there." That was the first indication I had of an enormous change in the heart of one Capanahua chief whose fellow tribesmen had breathed hate and promise of revenge for a long time.

In 1981 the chief of the Matses took advantage of a flight from his region to become acquainted with Yarinacocha and Pucallpa. He remained for two weeks. Since I was director of the Institute and not able to live with the Capanahua at that time, I accompanied him on the return flight because the plane would pass over the airstrip of the Capanahua. I was to be dropped off at the Capanahua village and picked up later.

We stopped at Buncuya, where the Capanahua live, and I forgot about the passengers in the airplane—Harriet and Hattie, the Matses chief, and his two sons—because the chief of the Capanahua came out to meet me. I started to greet him in a formal manner because the Capanahua do not show much emotion. If a son has been gone for many years and returns home, the father says, "You have returned, Son," and nothing more. The son replies, "Yes, Father, I have returned."

But this was a special moment for me to be able to meet him, so I embraced him. Then I remembered the passengers. I looked back at the airplane. To my alarm, the chief of the Matses had gotten out and was standing beside it. I said to the chief of the Capanahua, "Brother, what do you think? This is your brother, the chief of the Matses."

"Oh, is that so?" He knew that that chief had a Capanahua woman who had been stolen. Suddenly he ran toward the Matses chief and gave him a big embrace, saying, "*Uhu.*" Running after him I said to the Matses, "Welcome, Brother. Come see our place. Welcome!" Our linguists interpreted.

The chief of the Matses stood rooted to the ground, knowing whose land he was standing on and the long tradition of hostility which there had been between the two groups. Then he began to speak. The girls and I translated, they from Matses, I into Capanahua:

"I am not so bad as many are. I do not go about stealing and killing. I did not steal the woman that I have." (He had received her secondhand.) That was the first peaceful contact between the two groups.

In 1982 the linguists translated for the Matses the little Epistle of Philemon in which the Apostle Paul says that he is writing to Philemon and sending back a runaway slave who had become a believer while listening to Paul in prison. Then he says, "Now I know that you are not going to receive this one as your property but as your brother."

The first copies were being circulated among the Matses, who now knew how to read. One night the chief, as was his custom, called the men to a sing-along meeting. After they had gathered, the chief was slow to begin. The others said, "We are all here."

"No, we are not all here yet." One young slave had not come. Those young slaves could not be accepted into full standing in the community with the adult Matses men. They remained outside the pale.

"We are all here," the others insisted. "Why should we wait for that slave?"

"Tonight we are going to wait for him," the chief insisted. The young man came. The chief had him stand up in the midst of them. Then he said to the rest, "Tonight, Sachin is going to lead the singing." As a symbol of the impact that this short Epistle had on his heart, the chief made this gesture and the slave was accepted as a full member of the community.

In October 1983 a Matses man had left his community to discover what life was like elsewhere and to work for money, buy a rifle, and return. He worked much but made no money. Before returning to his village he took a canoe trip to a Capanahua community to visit. His own place was three hundred kilometers away. He had a conversation with a young Capanahua who had been with our people in Yarinacocha. They tell me that he said, "Previously we went about killing and stealing, but we no longer do that because the Word of God has come to our village. Now we live right."

This second peaceful contact between the two groups had as its basis the recognition by both groups of the message of love and brotherhood brought to them by the Word of God.

You Have Made Peru More Peruvian

Translation of a speech by the Minister of Education of Peru, The Honorable Jose Guabloche Rodriguez, on the occasion of the dedication of five New Testaments in Peru in 1979.

Dear Brothers in Christ, Monsignor Ariz brought us his blessing on a human work with a divine purpose, and the engineer asked that we not fail Peru, that we continue to follow God, responding to Him as He wants us to respond. I do not know exactly what you hope from me. I believe that my course of action has been spelled out by Jim Wroughton. He said that not only as Minister of Education but primarily as Pepe, your friend, he who has the honor and good fortune to know you these many years, I should speak.

And he also brought to mind the following: Three days ago was my birthday, and as Minister of Education I participated in a simple ceremony with the personnel who work in the Ministry of Education. The director general, General Rivas, who presided, presented to me three people: Pepe Guabloche—the friend; Jose Guabloche—General of Army; and Jose Guabloche—Minister of Education. He spoke eloquent words, very stirring words, to refer to each one of these three people. Since that day, that is to say since the eighteenth, I have thought much about the things he mentioned.

Although it may be questioned, Jose Guabloche has always concerned me. I have always worked on him and always tried to make of him the human being that I want him to be. This is because I know that he is called to be as human as he can possibly be with the help of God and with the help of his brothers in Christ.

So I thank you and repeat the feelings which are rising in me here because God is here. He is here not only in His Word, as

Monsignor Ariz said, but also in His full presence in the spirit of each one of you, whether in the form of music by the Murk family, whether in the form of a technical linguistic speech by Eugene Loos, in the stirring words of an apostle who has the courage to proclaim his faith as the engineer has done, or in the reading of the Word of God in their own languages as has been done by our Capanahua, Chayahuita, Amuesha, Huitoto, and Cashibo brethren just a few moments ago.

As your friend

I had noticed some time ago five books which had been provided for the Piros, Campas, Machiguengas, Aguarunas, and Huambisas. These, together with five before us today, add up to ten. But you tell me that more than one hundred have been done throughout the world, that is, for all humanity. I too sincerely believe, as Monsignor Ariz has said, that possibly the greatest work, or perhaps the only work which we should do, is to proclaim the Word of God, and not only with words coming out of our lips but also by every action, by every gesture, by every work we carry out. Sincere persons, honest persons, when they express themselves with words from the heart, and when they speak heart to heart, understand every word spoken, whatever the language may be in which it is spoken and whoever the person may be who speaks. I therefore, as Pepe Guabloche, as your friend and a friend of all those who are here present, thank you for the deference with which you have treated me, for the advice which you have always given me, and above all for the example of Christian life which you have demonstrated to me and of which I am very envious. I believe that this kind of envy is not sinful. It is entirely acceptable.

As the military man

Jose Guabloche, the military man, wants to thank you in the name of the armed forces and of all that is meant by the force needed by a nation to defend what it loves and what it appreciates through its faith in the grandeur of these people. I want to thank you on behalf of the armed forces for that which you have done for us Peruvians, for that which you have done with these our brothers who now with their emotions can express themselves through their own Scripture in their own language. In this way their history will not be read just by others and not be merely recited orally by themselves as traditions of the old men to the children. Now we can use a more direct and more concrete language to make ourselves understood and to make plain what this fatherland is in which they are a substantive part. It is wonderful that this is happening in the jungle, because its inhabitants are a great people in spite of the fact that some doubt that it is possible to live well in the jungle or for anything good to come from the jungle.

As education minister

As Minister of Education, I believe that you expect something. As a minister of this nation, in the name of the government, I convey the warmest, most sincere, and most stirring recognition which I can give you for the work which you are carrying out with the Word of God in the goodness of your hearts, with the lives which you have dedicated for many years to discovering the glories of the Indians. You have been doing much to make Peru more Peruvian. I know that these five groups, plus the previous ones to which the New Testament was given, are now being incorporated into our nation and through this into our history in accord with our concept of history. By means of the Gospel which they read in their own language they will direct their lives not only with the hope which the Gospel gives us, but also by participating in all the grandeur and dimensions of the Christian culture which is ours. All this will make Peru greater. All this will make us feel more Peruvian.

Therefore I repeat, in the name of the government, the only detail which remains is for me to say thank you for all that you give us and for all that you do for our Peru. I say this not only in the human dimension but also in the Peruvian dimension because, as Millie Lyon says, she is proud to be Peruvian and is happy when she sings our national anthem.

I believe that in this meeting we are reaching many goals. I should like to refer to the final words of Monsignor Ariz that, of all we undertake, this work is the only enduring one. If we do it, I believe that we can say with optimism and with assurance that even the very best of all past epochs was not as good as this. This one now beginning is going to be better, because the people who follow us will base their actions on our example and on our undertaking. We are very sure that the things they do will also be greater because God wants it that way, and in His name we seek to work. So, Pepe Guabloche, Jose Guabloche—general of the army, and Jose Guabloche—Minister of Education, join together in saying thank you, and may God bless you.

Vitality from the Vernacular
Cameron Townsend

Thirty-three years ago today I was in the city of Patzcuaro in Mexico when the first Inter-American Indian Congress closed its session and set up the Inter-American Indian Institute. General Lazaro Cardenas, president of the republic of Mexico, himself part Indian and very proud of it, was on the platform and gave the main address. The goal that was set before the representatives from many countries of Latin America, the United States, and Canada was to give to the minority language groups of the entire hemisphere the opportunity to learn to read in their own mother tongue, and then the national tongue of each country, whether it was Spanish, Portuguese, or English. It was a great day.

I will never forget a woman in Ecuador, from the area where Mary and Orville Johnson work. After they had labored there for eight years, this woman accepted Christ; three months later she stood up in a meeting that Elaine had arranged before we left Limoncocha. Several Indians testified. This same woman said, "For three months, ever since I let the Lord Jesus into my heart, I have been free from the demons. Not one has been able to bother me." Today it is my understanding that eighty-five percent of the people of her language group have turned to the Lord.

Also, in other parts of the world, learning to read their own languages has turned minority groups into vital forces.

I have visited the Caucasus four times and have seen people who fifty years ago were divided. They had their own old customs, which generally included fighting one another and neighboring groups and carrying out vengeance. But there were no books, no opportunities to obtain instruction that would make them vital forces in the life of their nations. Then, through bilingual education, they received that opportunity. Today we see the results. They speak two languages. They have not done away with their own language at all. They have used their own language as a means of obtaining a knowledge of the national language. And they continue to speak it; they continue to be proud of it. There are a hundred different languages in the Caucasus, roughly speaking. And the people are proud of them all. Bilingual education has opened the door to minority language groups so that they have gone to the top.

Is it worth it? Do you want to do that for just a handful of people? I know dedicated, competent, able Christians who are pastors of churches that number maybe two hundred members, and almost all of the two hundred have already heard the gospel. Most of them, or a good percentage of them, are already Christians, and yet the pastors are willing to shepherd that flock, week in and week out. Would you be willing to go to a minority group back in the jungles of Amazonia that numbers only two hundred and fifty people, in whose language the Bible does not exist, in whose situation there is no security for you and for whom you have to give up friends and possessions?

Determined Dorsi

Peter and Sue Westrum

The local government officers in our Kecamatan in Indonesia, together with leaders in the Berik community, worked with us to choose potential students to join the first adult literacy classes to be held in various villages along the Tor River among the Berik people. Our nextdoor neighbor, Dorsi, was a woman who had not impressed us as one desiring to learn. Besides, she had a newborn baby and a two-year-old constantly at her side.

We secretly hoped that she would not be one of those chosen to attend the first classes. And she was not. We breathed a sigh of relief. But Dorsi had other intentions. She came to the classroom the first day of classes anyway, baby at her breast and toddler tugging on her dress. She came every day and later brought her husband too.

To our amazement, Dorsi turned out to be the best student in the class and quickly learned the skill of reading and writing. She had a large family to feed, she had a house and garden to take care of, she had two children completely dependent on her at all times; yet she overcame all obstacles to learn to read and write because she had a desire to do so, even though neither we nor the local leaders recognized her potential.

Double Duty at the Duplex

Katherine Voigtlander and Thelma Johnston

On a dusty street corner in Tulancingo, Mexico, stands a sturdy duplex, one half of it the home of translators Katie Voigtlander and Artemisa Echegoyen. A chilly early morning hour may find Artie, her hat pulled over her ears, on the roof hanging wet laundry and Katie sweeping from the front walk the ubiquitous dirt and trash which has blown from the dump across the street.

But that is a small part of the story. Literacy work is their project: primers and a dictionary to promote bilingual education and the consequent opportunity for the Eastern Otomis to read their own New Testament, completed by Katie and Artie in 1974. Until they can read it, having the New Testament in their own language will not do the Eastern Otomis much good.

Even before Katie had finished her task of preparing the Museum of the Alphabet at JAARS in Waxhaw, North Carolina, she and Artie realized that providing a place for their Otomi friends to stay overnight would have wonderful results. They were right. Tulancingo is halfway between Mexico City or the state capital Pachuca and their village. As the Otomis travel to either place on business, they now have a comfortable place to stay, with supper and breakfast provided.

The breakfast hour finds either hostess knocking on the door of the other half of the duplex. "Good morning! How many of you are there today?" Hopefully there is enough food on hand—usually eggs, beans, and tortillas—without having to wait for the neighborhood store to open. Then at suppertime other Otomis may have arrived to spend the night—and they are hungry too!

"Today's schedule: nine for supper, four for breakfast," Katie recently wrote. "Our Jose came with his wife; he has just been married and says he will be baptized in April. We trust he has given up his drinking. Eulogio came and reported he is teaching reading and writing of their own language to the adults and teenagers of his church in San Antonio. Emiliano and Cornelio are teaching a similar class of adults in San Gregorio, interrupted last summer by field work. Cornelio is a student from Emiliano's first class of reading and writing Otomi in San Antonio. He never had the opportunity to finish first grade, but now he is teaching reading and writing in Otomi, a language far harder than Spanish, which is taught in public schools. Ila, one of Emiliano's students at San Antonio, is teaching two women there who had never been to school. It is going slowly, but they are persistent and doing better now that they have glasses!"

Anything can happen at the duplex. "Yesterday about 10 a.m. a truck pulled up in front of our house and one of our teacher friends, Maximino, rang the doorbell. He had brought various relatives and his wife, who had just had a miscarriage and needed attention; he wondered what to do or where to go. I directed them to the General Hospital and they rushed her there. After she leaves the hospital she will need to rest here for a few days before taking the four-hour truck ride back to San Antonio over that rough road," continued Katie.

The duplex has proved to be a marvelous opportunity for encouraging the Eastern Otomis from San Antonio, where Artie and Katie spent several years translating the New Testament, and from other nearby towns. Individual problems, family events, physical and spiritual needs appear in the conversations at the duplex. Katie and Artie seize every free moment to share the Gospel with their Otomi Indian friends and to motivate interest in the use of their own New Testament; they use it for devotions with whoever has a little time after breakfast or supper.

B.

Approach the task scientifically.

In the Nick of Time

Lester Troyer

A new man had just been appointed to the post of Acting Secretary of Education by the president. We had met him several times before, when he was serving in a lower office within the system. Since we had a policy matter that needed attention, I decided it was a good time to get an appointment and "kill two birds with one stone": convey our congratulations and talk about the policy issue with our Philippine branch.

His appointment secretary told me that the secretary was very busy preparing to leave in a few hours for Paris, France, for a top-level UNESCO meeting. At best I could expect only a minute or so of his time. When I was ushered into his ornate office, I found the place a beehive of activity: underlings were scurrying around looking for papers and dictating notes to secretaries while aides were packing papers and files into briefcases.

I had barely greeted him when he interjected, "Oh, Mr. Troyer, you are a godsend. I am supposed to present copies of materials that we have produced for our literacy programs here in the Philippines when I give my speech in Paris. I am desperate! I do not have a ghost of an idea what we have done or what is available. Could you SIL people please help me out? It is going to be very embarrassing for me to give that talk and then have nothing to back it up!"

He was leaving in a couple of hours. I was downtown. We did not have enough material in our small office to represent the work we had done in order to give a complete and impressive picture.

How to get adequate information to the secretary in time was the question. "May we airmail it to you, sir?" I asked.

"Yes, yes, by all means. It should get there in time if you get it off this evening," he said. I rushed off. The policy matter must wait for another time and another day. I hurried back to our Manila group house where we had most of our material. With the help of our staff there, we readied a bundle and shipped it off that afternoon post haste to Paris, France.

Two weeks later when the secretary returned, he thanked me profusely for our help. "When the time came for me to make my speech at the international forum there in Paris, I got up with no materials to back up my talk. During my speech the doors of the auditorium opened and my aides brought in the stack of readers and primers in our Philippine languages that you had sent. I used them to demonstrate what our government is doing in literacy. No one from any other country represented there had a display like the one we from the Philippines had. It arrived in the nick of time. We are very grateful to you for your help!"

Again God's perfect timing saved the day. It was a privilege for us to be able to serve this official and his government. It was a blessing for them to feel, even though we had done most of the hard spade work, that it was *their* work and program. That is the way it must always be; after all, SIL is only a servant. Part of being a successful, fulfilled, and happy servant is being able to remain in the shadows.

Scientific Organization

Cameron Townsend

SIL is primarily a scientific organization. I do not refer to the motives, but to the work. When you produce a grammar and a dictionary, it is possible that nobody in the tribe will ever use them. Some university professors may have them on their shelves. But you must put in all that work, fifteen years or more, just figuring out how the language is put together. That is important, because you are going to translate the Bible.

So you work, labor, struggle, and take special courses; you talk with experts—this is scientific work with a purpose. A man who volunteers to be a medical missionary can belong to a medical society at the same time. It is strictly scientific, but he needs it for his medical profession. In linguistics, you must be a linguist, at least as regards the language you are assigned to, and that means years of study and effort. Not missionary work, but scientific work. So we are received, even in the USSR, because we are the Summer Institute of Linguistics. We want to use the fact of our being recognized as scientists to get God's Word translated, not only into the languages of the USSR that have never had it, but into every language of the world.

I think it is extremely important to do a scientific job, not just for the sake of science, but to do a proper translation. We praise God for the men and women whom God has raised up to become outstanding linguists, doing a scientific job, not just for Bible translation, but also to help people out of their cultural isolation by reaching them in their own tongues. Then these linguistic groups are incorporated into the life of the nation. Doors are opened to us in high circles because we specialize in Indian languages and have a scientific organization, SIL!

God is love. If we are to follow Him, we must love one another. That is why SIL is endeavoring to learn all of the languages of the world that have never yet been written. There are over three thousand still waiting for study. And that is why we want to give them, along with an alphabet, along with primers, along with dictionaries and grammars, along with bilingual education, some portion of the greatest book of history, the Word of God. They have a right to have it.

Let us advance with our two organizations, SIL and WBT. Other organizations can be formed which will concentrate on Bible translation, or church-building, or medical work, but we must put special emphasis on the science of linguistics because God has led us in that way. As God has led us thus far to victory after victory, He will continue to lead. Nothing today is any harder or any more dangerous than what faced us before. The Lord says go, go to every creature. We can go, we have gone, we will continue to go, and we will encourage others to go—that the goal will be reached and our Lord will return!

Scientific Approach

Cameron Townsend

We follow what we call the linguistic approach. That means we go to a man through his soul gate, through his own language. We want to learn the languages, and we might as well go about it in a scientific way. If we are going to be linguists, we should be good linguists!

God has blessed us with men who can teach our people to be scientific about our work. When we do this, governments are glad to have our help. Universities welcome us, help us, and respect our work. Then when someone comes along saying, "Those folks are giving the Bible to the Indians," the answer of the scientists is, "They are doing a scientific job. They are analyzing those languages. They are writing articles and books that are valuable to linguistic science."

We want to give an alphabet to every linguistic group. We want to analyze the grammar of their languages. We want to form dictionaries for linguistic science. But above all, we want to give people some of the best literature of history, the Bible. We feel that each group has a right to that spiritual treasure.

We must do a good linguistic job, producing a Bible that is translated accurately, as close to the original as we know how, as well as grammatically correct in the vernacular language. Then people will listen to us, as we speak both of linguistics and of our Lord and Savior Jesus Christ.

Therefore, you Bible translators, when academic people are giving lectures, attend them as a matter of courtesy. When you see in a newspaper that there is a scientific meeting, attend it. Invite local scholars into your homes, listen to their talk, attend their lectures, join their scientific societies, be present at their open sessions, publish articles, publicize their scientific contributions. It is vitally important for us to stick to the scientific linguistic approach.

Race to the Swift?

Richard Pittman

It was an unequal race. One of the runners had already been in his host country a good number of years. He already had property there and a school for Indians. He also had the inside track with those who sponsored both runners. He was much in demand for speaking at churches, schools, missionary meetings, and Bible conferences. His eloquence and credibility were very high. He had a son of great promise who could already speak one of the Indian languages and who was preparing to do Bible translation for it.

The other runner was not yet known in the host country. Nor was he well known in the groups which send and support runners. He had started far behind in the race, and he did not, in fact, have the kind of eloquence which gave the first runner such a competitive edge. And though a brilliant young man had married his niece, he too was far behind the first runner's son, who could speak both the national and an Indian language.

There were some who thought that Runner Two should hit the church, school, mission-meeting circuit. But he eschewed widespread publicity in the homeland, calling rather on host country academics and officials, querying, conferring, asking advice on Indian problems, needs, aspirations, and offering the services of linguists and literacy workers to help the government meet its obligations to its own minority groups. He encouraged his nephew and others to do the same.

It did not look promising. At first he seemed to fall even further behind. Runner One both kept and widened his lead. Many of the host government officials and academics to whom Runner Two related were not declared believers. Some were of political persuasions far different from those of friends at home. Runner Two was sometimes criticized, therefore, for time he spent with them and for admiration he bestowed on them. It was said that he ought to be spending his time with believers.

But while Runner One's credibility with his home constituency was growing, Runner Two was establishing his credibility with the government and university people in the host country. When visas were needed they became progressively easier to get. Visas for the team of Runner One became agonizingly difficult to obtain. His team, in fact, never did grow beyond a small handful.

Bible translation had been a declared purpose of both Runners. The son of Runner One did some. The nephew of Runner Two completed a New Testament and helped train thousands of others to translate. By 1995 Team Two had more than 420 published New Testaments resulting from their work.

It is history and a parable. It does not detract from the sovereignty of God to recognize some ways in which He works. Having entrusted administration of nations to their own citizens, He holds them responsible for the way they rule their fellow men and tells all men to be subject to them. In language matters, however, many do not know what to do. Expatriates who do know and who are patient and humble enough to take the time required to earn credibility in lands where they want to work will be rewarded with permits.

It is wonderful to be accredited at home. It is absolutely essential, however, to be accredited abroad. Those at home eventually learn that success abroad comes when guests earn the trust of their hosts.

Please Care ...about Attending Scientific Meetings

Cameron Townsend

When academic people are giving lectures, we should attend as a matter of courtesy. When we see in a newspaper that there is a scientific meeting, we should attend. When a missionary read, in 1935, of a scientific meeting which was to be held in Mexico City, he drew it to my attention. I attended and met a former rector of the University of Mexico and the Minister of Labor. Both of them helped us as a result of our attending an academic meeting.

Some do not care to do this. Please care! Please cultivate! Have these scholars into your homes. Listen to them talk. Attend their lectures. Join their scientific societies. Publish articles in their journals, recognizing their scientific contributions. We tried to do this from the beginning, publishing, since 1937, in Mexican journals.

In host countries SIL aviation personnel should attend aviation meetings, radio personnel should attend radio club meetings, medical personnel should attend medical society meetings, education-related personnel should attend education conferences.

Who knows how God will use these caring contacts?

Cultural Identity Rescued

Translation of a speech of Mr. Jose Castaneda Medinilla, director of the National Indian Institute of Guatemala, at the closing ceremony December 19, 1980, of a course in applied linguistics taught by SIL in the highlands of Guatemala.

In the agreement signed in 1959 between the government of Guatemala and the Summer Institute of Linguistics there was stipulated, among other things, the great importance of doing studies of the Maya languages of Guatemala.

It is very satisfying to have evidence that right through the time of their stay in Guatemala, members of the Summer Institute of Linguistics have fully lived up to their promises regarding that scientific work. Their investigations have revealed the typical phonetic and morphological characteristics of the majority of the languages descended from classical Maya.

Such careful study has succeeded in rescuing from oblivion a large part of that linguistic treasure. This rescue contributes beyond doubt to the maintenance of the cultural identity of the groups who live in our rural areas.

An eloquent demonstration of this is the development of this course in bilingual education which has brought into focus problems and aspects of the vernacular languages. A relevant aspect is that the descriptions and analyses presented have been designed for practical application and not as a purely scientific exercise.

This labor of applied linguistics is the best contribution which the Summer Institute of Linguistics has given to the Guatemalan culture. It has permitted not only the maintenance but in fact the improvement of the collaboration which happily exists between that organization and the National Indian Institute.

For that reason I consider it necessary to express in a very justified way the congratulations of the National Indian Institute to the organizers and the participants in this cultural achievement. This course, in addition to other good results, has the effect of awakening the conscience regarding both human and scientific values which are enshrined in this linguistic treasure house. This should be considered a source of pride for all of us who dream of the consolidation of a bicultural Guatemala in which all manifestation of social or ethnocultural discrimination has disappeared.

I repeat, in conclusion, that the National Indian Institute recognizes the scientific activities of the Summer Institute of Linguistics in our midst as being extremely valuable, especially because of the scarcity of technically trained personnel in this area. The National Indian Institute regards the Summer Institute of Linguistics as its best partner and as an ally in the fight to save in every way possible the cultural identity of the Maya groups.

Visit-a-critic Year

Kenneth Gregerson

Dear Colleagues,

Half a century ago Uncle Cam began teaching linguistics and taking it abroad to serve deep social and spiritual needs of cultural minorities. Looking around at present—fifty years later—I am filled with admiration for all that you under God are doing in fulfillment of this shared vision for SIL.

My purpose in writing you today is to encourage you to keep doing the great job that you have been doing in making new friends and in saying thank you to old friends where you are.

In March and April I will be visiting linguists and their departments in Denmark, Sweden, Norway, and Finland to give linguistic talks and build friendships. A number of our members-in-training are studying at those universities and some of their professors are interested in the languages SIL is working on. Later in 1984 I plan to make other visits in Washington, DC, with diplomats from countries where SIL serves.

Please continue to maintain academic and other professional contacts. Reference to the fiftieth anniversary of SIL may not be important in academia, but please make every effort to reach out. Let me suggest some ways to do this:

Lectures at universities or scholarly societies are excellent for building rapport. Inviting lectures on the part of other scholars at our workshops, courses, etc., is equally recommended. How about pushing this year to get that paper published in some journal? I suggest writing a letter or paying a visit to give out a reprint or book of interest to another scholar.

Coauthoring a volume or paper with another non-SIL person of similar interests is very good. Administrators and senior consultants can encourage selected people to get to local and international professional conferences—and even give a paper. Consider starting a local monthly linguistic meeting for members and local linguists to give papers and discuss things.

All of our professionals need to reach out, whether linguists or pilots, printers, computer people, workers in community development, etc. While most of the effective contacts will need to be built out of local materials to meet local needs, we stand ready to support you in any special materials you may need, such as the SIL annual report, SIL seal for official letters, and a special film called "Between Two Worlds."

III

THIRD CONCERN: THE PEOPLE

The secret behind all SIL relationships and language achievements is LOVE of friends, neighbors, enemies.

———————

———————

Cameron Townsend:

I have asked people at our translation centers to visit the workmen from the surrounding area. And not only the workmen but the luminaries in the region too. People feel honored when a foreign visitor comes to call on them.

———————

Oh, how important it is to cultivate friendship, to meet with people, to dine with them, to get them to understand our point of view, to put ourselves at their orders, and to have them feel that we look up to them and honor them!

———————

Love means to recognize the other fellow, to recognize his importance, to recognize him as someone to serve, to respect, to honor... When we show love, people listen. And love includes going to their meetings, going to the meetings of scientific groups, to the groups who are studying the future of the people we work with... Love is the badge. "By love serve one another."

A.

Be a friendly neighbor.

Better than Cake!

Robert Griffin

"Your wife's bread is better than cake!" Perhaps that is why Ecuador's Minister of Treasury visited us often. He liked that jungle home-baked bread.

A delightful person, the minister was young, enthusiastic, and one who would cross a street in Quito to greet us if he saw us on the other side. We became great friends. About once every two months he would come out to the jungle to spend a weekend. In addition to filling up on Louise's delicious bread, he enjoyed alligator hunting. We'd go out at night in a dugout canoe with a flashlight. Alligators' eyes reflect the beam of light and shine like the brakelights on a Ford.

Another diplomatic friendship I was privileged to enjoy in Ecuador was with our U.S. ambassador, Christian Ravendal. He had been very happy in his former assignment in Hungary; he loved the Hungarians, learned their language, and spoke it well. When Hungary was overrun, he had to leave. He grieved for and sorely missed his Hungarian friends. Often I picked him up in Quito with the Helio and took him to the jungle to spend the weekend with us.

One day as we stood gazing out across our little jungle lake, impulsively he hugged me and said, "Bob, you don't know what it means to come out here to be with you dear, godly people."

When we first went to Ecuador we were based in Shell Mera. I became acquainted with the military commander there, Major Rio Frio. The major had charge of the entire eastern area of the country, a very sensitive post because Peru and Ecuador were in dispute over the boundary between the two countries.

We became good friends with this man and his family, close enough to tease one another. When you are able to do that cross-culturally, the relationship is going well. He enjoyed teasing me about my gringo-Spanish—why didn't I speak it as well as my children did? Our children frequently played with his. In fact, if Louise could not find ours, she would soon locate them at the major's house. They liked the food there better than at home.

One day I sensed that the major was troubled. After some small talk he asked, "Don Roberto, I wonder, is it possible that you could help me?"

"Certainly, if I am able. What is your need?"

"I have men on our outposts on the frontier with Peru who are living off the land—on bananas, papaya, and yucca, the things they can grow. I send rice, beans, sugar, salt, all those staples, down the river in dugout canoes, only to have them capsize in the rapids so all is lost. This has happened time and time again. I am at my wit's end. My men are not doing well because I cannot get food to them. Could you fly it to them?"

I was surprised by the request. To gain time to think I asked, "Are there airstrips at each of these locations?"

"We will make them!" he promised.

"Let me think about it," I answered. "I will have an answer for you in a day or so." I could not tell him, but I was in a dilemma with no one to consult. It was not the type of subject I could talk about on the radio with our director in Quito. What should I do? Should I serve the Ecuadorian military with this missionary plane? What will the people who donated the money to put the airplane here to serve missionaries think? How will my supporters react—those dear people who are making it possible for us to live in Ecuador and be missionaries? What will they think of my flying food to the Ecuadorian military? Is this what they are supporting me to do? Thoughts like that paraded through my mind.

Finally, after Louise and I prayed over it, we concluded that the Lord Jesus emphasized He came not to be served, but to be a servant. I realized that servanthood was my role: in this case, to serve the major in his important need. We decided that we had been called to be servants to all, not just to the missionaries.

The next day I found the major to advise him of my decision. He was delighted. Within hours his men were backing their 6x6 trucks up to our hangar and unloading mountains of bags filled with salt, beans, rice, and sugar. I looked at that pile and at my little six-passenger airplane and winced. I had just promised to fly all that stuff out to the jungle! And I knew this was only the beginning. I would be making a lot of flights.

The major was as good as his word. They hacked airstrips out of the jungle as he promised, and a lot of people were happy every time I arrived at the various outposts. After about a year of my pioneering effort and the lengthening of the airstrips, the major was able to get help from his own air force and I was happily out of a job. During those days I had made many good friends by flying those mercy missions.

The day came—and this is the thrilling end result of my willingness to be a servant—when the major was assigned to Quito. He came to me in tears to tell me of his change of command. He loved his men, he loved his command, and he loved the Oriente where he had been for several years. He did not want to leave but knowing he must follow orders, he said, "I have to go. Don Roberto, would you please be the one to carry me to Quito?"

"I am honored," I said. "I am deeply touched that you should ask me. I will be pleased to help you, but I am saddened to see you leave." As I said this I knew he had four other means of transport to leave Shell Mera: the Ecuadorian Air Force, a local jungle airline that came out of Quito twice a week, by road in a military vehicle, or in a private vehicle. He chose to ask me to fly him because of our friendship.

The departure was a tender and sad moment which I will never forget. I loaded his baggage in the airplane while all his staff officers gathered around to say their goodbyes. There were lots of tears. Both the major and his men showed the evidence of much love and comradeship.

With cheeks still wet with our tears, we took off on our way into the highlands through a narrow pass in the mountains and finally leveled off at 13,000 feet, headed north toward Quito. It was then the major turned to me and said, "Don Roberto, I've been wondering for a long time—I want to ask you something." Then, in essence, he asked, "What makes you tick?"

That is called a leading question! In about ten minutes I explained my relationship to Jesus Christ and my calling to Ecuador to be a servant to him and the people of that lovely land. The tears welled up in his eyes and started rolling down his cheeks again. Grabbing my arm, he squeezed it and said, "Don Roberto, that's what I want!" And easily, quickly, with some help from me he took title to a mansion in glory.

That was a glorious moment, but it took three years of building a friendship and of being a servant to that man to gain the credibility for that conversation and his step of faith.

Air Base Commander
without an Airplane

Merrill Piper

Near the start of the SIL work in Peru the Peruvian government established an air base in Pucallpa. But since they had no aircraft to place there, they put the facility under the command of a second lieutenant.

Not long after he arrived, an important conference of high-ranking Peru Air Force officers was called in Iquitos, five-and-a-half hours flying time by small plane downriver from Pucallpa. The second lieutenant was invited, but nothing was budgeted to enable him to go.

Attempts to charter a small plane failed because he had no money to pay. Providentially, he was able to explain his predicament to Uncle Cam. "SIL will be delighted to fly you to Iquitos," replied Uncle Cam.

Merrill Piper was assigned to fly him in the tiny Aeronca Sedan which now hangs from the rafters of the hangar at JAARS.

He not only flew him down but also remained overnight to fly him back the next day.

Footnote: The second lieutenant became a Peruvian Air Force general.

A Sunday Servant

Robert Griffin

"Bob, can you bring him home? We have to get him out of there; we have to bring him home." Ken Maryott was talking about his *datu*—his tribal chief—whom I had picked up a week earlier, deathly ill with malaria and other complications.

When I flew the frail little old man to the Baptist clinic in Malaybalay, Ken and I had despaired of his life. In fact, I was certain that in a few days I would be flying the body home in a shroud. But, after only a week of heavy doses of vitamins and malaria medicine, the transformation was miraculous. He seemingly was cured of all but one illness, one for which there was no medicine—homesickness. The *datu* was agonizingly and frantically begging to go home.

I wanted to serve him, but the only free slot in my heavy schedule was Sunday. Normally we guarded that as a day of rest and worship. However, I had no choice. If I carried the *datu* home it would have to be on Sunday. I told Ken I would make the flight.

It was one of those deliciously crisp, clear tropic mornings when he climbed into the plane beside me, grinning from ear to ear, his joy to be going home contagious. I rejoiced to be flying on such a beautiful day and was glad I could make him so happy. But for me it was just another routine take-the-*datu*-home trip. I could not have guessed how God was planning to use this Sunday mercy flight.

An hour or so later the *datu*, totally captivated by his bird's-eye view, was gazing in wonder at the steaming crater on top of 10,000-foot Mount Apo when a surprising call came on the radio from translator Gordon Svelmoe. "Bob, we have a real sick boy here. We do not know what is wrong, and nothing we do seems to help. Would it be possible for you to come by our place on the way back?"

"Of course, Gordon, I'll be glad to," I answered, memories of their happy, vibrant four-year-old filling my mind. "I should be there by the middle of the afternoon."

Soon I bade goodbye to the *datu*, who thanked me with another big toothless grin and a hug. We had become buddies. It is surprising how love can communicate without words.

As I turned north and climbed for altitude I began wondering: Would the Svelmoes be able to meet me at the airstrip? What would I do if they were not there? I knew they had a long, hard trip just to get there. Their village area was too hilly for an airstrip so they faced an hour's walk to the nearest road and two hours of dusty jouncing on hard board seats in a bus that kept an erratic schedule. Some days it did not run at all. I wondered if all the pieces of that puzzle would fit together. But they did! I had not been on the ground ten minutes when I saw a roostertail of dust chasing a dilapidated taxi up the access road. That taxi "just happened" to be waiting at the crossroads where Thelma, cradling Paul in her arms, got down from the bus.

I shall never forget holding the limp rag doll that was little Paul while Thelma climbed into the plane. He was unconscious, his eyes rolled back, the slow rise and fall of his chest the only indicator of life. Would we make it in time? It was more than an hour's flight to medical help.

About fifteen minutes out of Nasuli I was starting to descend. "Where are you going to land, Bob?" Thelma asked anxiously. We had two options: our translation center at Nasuli or the clinic about six minutes beyond, where we had a little airstrip and I could taxi nearly to the back door. It was there just after dawn that I had picked up the Sangir *datu*.

"Well, I think we ought to go right to the clinic."

Her musing answer, "That will be ten or twelve more minutes of total flying time," told me she was thinking about the cost.

"Money is not a concern at this point," I said. "We're going to take him to the clinic just as quickly as possible." As I taxied in,

Dr. Linc Nelson and two nurses met us and carried Paul immediately into the clinic, Thelma trailing anxiously behind them.

Next day I saw the doctor. "Bob," he told me, "if you had not gotten Paul here yesterday, I do not think he would have made it. He was in a deep diabetic coma. We caught it just in time."

What a God-directed chain of events! If the *datu* had not been "climbing the wall" to go home, we would not have made the flight and there would have been no radio communication available on Sunday. But I was already in the air with the radio in use when Gordon heard me. But why did Gordon even turn on his radio? He knew we did not have any Sunday radio standby. I do not know, but I believe God ordained all those events so I could pick up little Paul.

It was another lesson to me and to all our aviation men that God expects us to be servants seven days of the week.

Oh, yes, Paul recovered. His diabetes was stabilized, and he grew to be a strapping young man.

No Arrangements Had Been Made

Millie Lyon

As you know, Floyd is president of the Rotary Club in the capital of the state of Peru where we live. It has been a trying job, yet we have felt that God led us into Rotary thirteen years ago to be a witness for Him. Thirteen years of building relationships, listening to earsplitting band music, attending midnight suppers of heavy food. We have missed more functions at our center than we have attended. It is hard living between two cultures. I am not trying to paint us as martyrs, for we dearly love these people and enjoy being with them. We have gotten weary in welldoing, I guess—but just lend an ear.

Friday was almost the last straw. We had the regular end-of-the-month supper with husbands and wives at the hotel. Floyd went to town Friday morning and found no arrangements had been made. He had to handle it all at a higher price because the cook had to work extra. This last-minute way of doing things or not doing them at all has been difficult.

Floyd was ready to quit! We have had months of the same thing; yet we know we are where God placed us, even with the heavy load we already carry. We went to the dinner taking two couples from the capital with us. We especially wanted one man to give his testimony. Jimmy did give his testimony to the forty people attending. (It was so rainy we expected only half that many.) He gave it as a national, as a Catholic businessman who had come to know the Lord just two years before. After he finished, he gave an invitation for those who wanted to be born again to raise their hands. Many shot up. Then he said, "Those who want to pray the prayer of accepting Christ, stand up." Almost everyone present did so. Fantastic sight!

How real was it? Only God knows. But afterwards a number talked with us. Yesterday at a noon birthday party we talked to several and found a lot of interest in spiritual things still. We invited them to come home with us, but our road was almost impassable. Ten did come in a pickup in spite of heavy rains.

One key couple have been vice-presidents this year and will be presidents beginning in July. They are determined to go on with the Lord. We spent three hours talking to them about the Bible, explaining it and suggesting ways for personal devotions.

There are prayer and testimony breakfasts in the national capital, and we are eager for one to start here. Pray for this small group of believers. They are civic leaders. They need teaching, commitment to a personal prayer life and Bible study, so pray often for them.

Dona Marta

Natalie Earp

The shrill jangle of the telephone cut through the cheerful conviviality of the Townsend home at Waxhaw, North Carolina, where Elaine was hosting one of her thrice-weekly ladies' salad luncheons. There was a radio message from Lima, from Yarinacocha: "Dona Marta just went to be with the Lord." Elaine felt weak and shaken, for even though Marta was 104 years old, she thought, Oh, one of my best prayer warriors, and she's gone!

Her mind raced back to a day in Peru thirty-two years earlier. Cameron had had to make a trip to the States, and Elaine and the four children had returned from Lima to Yarinacocha in time for school to begin. Arriving at their home, they found a frail, sickly-looking, shriveled-up little old lady—a leper—waiting. She explained that someone had told her that Elaine could tell her the way to heaven. Would she do that, please?

Oppressive heat and jungle humidity had taken their toll on the children, who were tired, fussy, and anxious to have a cold drink and get unpacked as soon as possible. But the Lord gave Elaine grace to realize the urgency of the situation. Putting everything else aside, she welcomed Marta Zaneuri into her home and shared Scriptures with her. Dona Marta made it easy to tell her that the Lord died for her and that she was included in His plan of salvation. She eagerly accepted Jesus as her Lord and Savior that day, and her heart was completely transformed.

Although she did not live in total isolation, Marta had few friends because of her leprosy, and there was no one who really cared for her. She had been living mostly on tobacco. Not only did she become new in Christ, but her eating habits changed and her health began to improve. She was not satisfied just knowing that her sins were forgiven; she wanted to learn to read God's Word for herself.

Elaine Townsend dearly loved to teach people to read. Before meeting and marrying Uncle Cam, she had been uniquely prepared for this ministry; in the Chicago school system she had supervised a number of schools devoted to training retarded children. Under her guidance and in collaboration with some Peruvian educators, primers had been prepared and bilingual teachers trained for several dozen schools throughout Peru's jungle area.

But for Dona Marta, the challenges seemed almost insurmountable. She was seventy-two years old at the time and her eyes were failing. Not only that, but she had to come by canoe across the lake in the hot sun about an hour each way. However, soon she was coming three or four times a week. Cameron was a little squeamish about the leprosy but Elaine was not.

Always when Dona Marta arrived, Elaine welcomed her with an embrace, and they shared a time of fellowship, singing hymns at the piano and enjoying coffee or cold lemonade and goodies at the table on the big screened porch where they held their reading lesson and Bible study. At noon Dona Marta went home, and the Townsends' lunch was served at that same table. Often Cameron thought, I really appreciate my wife's love for this lady, but what if we all catch leprosy?

In spite of the difficulties involved, Dona Marta progressed rapidly, both in her ability to read and in her understanding of the Scriptures. She had no electricity in her home, and in the daytime she had to work in her fields. So at night she poured some oil into a little can, put a cloth wick in it, and studied by this light. Because her eyes were very poor, someone got her some magnifying glasses, but eventually she could not see even with those. However, she was a diligent student and within three months she was reading. One of the first things she wanted to learn was the books of the Bible so that she could find her way around.

One day Elaine and Marta were reading together in the fifth chapter of Matthew. "Love your enemies, bless those who curse you, do good to those who hate you, and pray for those who despitefully use you, and persecute you."

Marta was aghast. "Dona Elena," she said, "is that the Lord talking?"

"Yes. Why?" answered Elaine.

"Well," she said, "ever since I've been a believer and I go to the meetings, my neighbors come when I'm gone; they open up the gate to my garden and let their animals in, and they eat all my vegetables. So when I get home, I go across the road and open up their gate and put my animals in their garden to get even with them. But if Jesus says to love your enemies, do good to those who despitefully use you, I cannot do that any more, can I?"

Elaine said, "That is right, Marta. You cannot." From that day on she never did that again.

Marta was a changed person, happy in her relationship with the Lord. She never tired of telling the story of God's love and salvation to anyone who would listen. Her favorite hymn was "Are you weary? Are you heavy-laden? Tell it to Jesus; tell it to Jesus." Until the end of her life Marta prayed daily for Elaine Townsend.

Cocoon in the Loam

Richard Pittman

There are advantages to walking barefoot in the jungle. First, you do not frighten the living creatures around you. Second, you see and hear more than you would if you were lumbering along in heavy boots.

Thus it was that on the day a Tawusay (which rhymes with "how say") villager was slipping through West Irian's Lakes Plains jungle, he saw—or heard—or sensed something different beside the path. Looking cautiously about him he saw a place where the earth had been disturbed. What could it mean? Both turtles and birds of certain species are known to dig nests for their eggs and cover them for incubation.

The fresh earth was so soft he could scoop it out with his hands. Sure enough, his fingers soon met with a leathery resistance. The object he uncovered, however, was not a clutch of eggs but a bark "cocoon." Peeling the bark back a bit, he realized he had found a newborn baby girl.

The finder knew that it was not uncommon for families who felt unable to provide for newborn babes to abandon or bury them in the jungle. He also knew that a family of outsiders in the village, with four girls of their own, had once saved a Tawusay child...

SIL's Mary Jane Munnings was indeed interested. Though the baby's eyes, ears, nose, and mouth were caked with dirt, and though she had a bad wound at the bridge of her nose and was too weak to cry or suck, she was breathing. As Mary Jane gently washed out the dirt, she could see that, aside from the wound, the child was without blemish.

As word of the foundling spread through the village, a Tawusay mother with a babe of her own offered to feed her. Since the baby was too weak to nurse, the surrogate mother expressed her own milk and dripped it, a few drops at a time, into the baby's mouth. By nightfall the infant was nursing on her own. The next day other nursing mothers came to take turns feeding the baby themselves. One week after the finding, the baby's own parents, reconsidering, decided they would like to keep her after all.

SIL is ethnophile!

Some Fellow-members
of the Cattlemen's Association
William Eddy

Along with Bible translation work comes opportunity to help Indian minorities in very tangible ways. One of the most satisfying experiences that I have had took place in February 1978, when I saw the titles to land presented to the Cofan and Secoya people of Ecuador by the government.

It started twenty years ago when we were building a home in Limoncocha. I suddenly had to leave there and go to Quito with a tooth problem. While I was sitting in the dental chair, my dentist said, "That is an exciting work you are doing out in the jungle. I would like to take my family out to see what is going on." My wife was on twenty-four hour nursing call, our four girls were growing up, and my home construction work was going on; so we really did not have much time. I did not see how we could entertain them. But he insisted, so I went back to Limoncocha and told Maxine that we would have guests the following weekend.

They came, but instead of staying for just a weekend, they were with us for a week because it rained and the airplane could not get back to Quito. So there we were, looking at each other across the table, running out of things to say; lots of work was being held up (I thought).

Twenty years later I found myself in a dental chair in the same office but with a different dentist. This time it was the son, who had been on that trip with his daddy and mother and sister to Limoncocha twenty years before. He had just graduated from high school back in 1959 and had received that trip from his dad as a graduation present.

When I went into his office this time, he said to me, "How are things going, Bill?"

I said, "Good for me, but not too good for those Indians."

He said, "What do you mean?"

I said, "They are about to lose their land." I explained how the oil companies had built roads out there and now people were flooding from the mountains to the jungle and were moving in on Indian land. There was danger that the Indians would lose that land.

He said, "But that cannot happen! They have got to have that land. When I was out there visiting your place, I saw that they are really dependent on their land. I followed Indian guides through the jungle; I rode in their canoes up the river. A letter must be written to the president. You wait. As soon as I am through with your tooth, I will write that letter."

He kept a lot of patients waiting in the outer office while he wrote a letter demanding that the Indians be given their constitutional right. I thanked him for it. Then I wondered just how I would get the letter to the president. I had tried to see the president for months but with no success.

A few days later I came back to my dentist friend, before his patients had started coming, early in the morning. "Victor," I said, "I do not know how to get this to the president. He is awfully busy." The dentist went right to the telephone and called someone named Arturo. Then I walked with Victor over to Arturo's office for a few minutes. As I walked through the door into his office, I noticed the sign above it said, "National Cattlemen's Association, President." Victor introduced me to Arturo, and Arturo heard that I was a JAARS mechanic, interested in the problems of the Indians.

Arturo said, "Bill, back when I was a little boy, my daddy had a missionary friend. He was working with the Auca people. I remember my daddy used to take me down on weekends to Shell Mera to visit with this missionary. He used to sit there and listen to him tell stories by the hour; I was right beside my daddy's knee. He said that man was later killed by those Indians. I have never forgotten the impression that I had of his love for those people and his desire to reach them at any cost. That man's name was Nate Saint."

"Victor," Arturo continued, "if there is any way I can help you, I sure want to. By the way, Ecuador's president is a member of the Cattlemen's Association and a good friend of mine."

I told him I was sure there was some way he could help. He told me to bring some Indians to the city so he could meet them.

A couple of weeks later they were there. He asked them right away if they would like to raise cattle. They said, "Yes. Game is getting hard to find, and we would, as a matter of fact, like to start raising cattle."

He said, "I'll give some to you. Would you like to be members of the Association?"

They did not know what that meant but they said, "Sure." So he had his secretary make out membership cards for the National Cattlemen's Association of Ecuador. While his secretary was putting the cards in plastic, he was on the phone calling the president's office. He explained to the president that some members of the Association were having a problem out in the Oriente and needed his help. The president said, "Come on over in the morning at 10:00."

So we had an appointment with the president at 10:00 the next morning. There in full regalia, feathers and all, were the chiefs and others; Bub Borman, translator, and I were there with them. The president was very understanding and promised that they would have their land. Just one week later a team of surveyors was out there running boundary lines for what turned out to be a 62,000-hectare grant of land for the Cofans and the Secoyas. It was a thrilling time. How was I to know, twenty years ago, that the sixteen-year-old boy was later going to go to the University of

Pittsburgh Dental School, get his degree, come back and take over his father's practice? His father retired and the son became my dentist. He knew Arturo, whose father had known and been impressed by Nate Saint. Arturo knew the president. All were so concerned about the Indians that they wanted to help.

Make the River Grind Your Wheat

Cameron Townsend

Service to all! Service in love, service in the name of Jesus Christ. Service to the enemy. The Old Testament makes it plain that a man was supposed to help his enemy by returning a stray ox. Christ said in Luke 6:27, "Do good to those who hate you." It is basic.

Stan Ford was one of our pioneers in Mexico. We sent him out to a town where the people had to go a day's journey to get to a mill to grind their wheat. If they had to wait, it meant a day to get there and a day to return—three days to get a sack of wheat ground into flour. Stan Ford knew a bit about mechanics, so he said to them, "Why don't you have the river grind your wheat into flour?"

"The river? How can the river do that?"

He told them how. They liked the idea and asked what it would cost.

Stan wrote to me in Mexico City. I went to the electrical commission of the government and said, "Would you like to help an Indian town?"

"Why, yes," they said, "that's what we are established for."

"Well, they need a water wheel. Can you get them one?"

They gave me the data and the price. I wrote the information to Stan. He got the people together and told them. They said, "Is that all it will cost? Why, we spend that much money every time we hold a feast for St. Anthony! We will let the saint go without a festival this year so we can use the money to get a wheel and a mill." Soon they were grinding their wheat at home, eliminating the loss of three days per man per trip, as well as the charge for grinding.

Then Stan asked them, "Why don't you have chairs and tables instead of squatting on logs on the floor?"

They said, "It's a lot of work to saw trees into boards."

Stan said, "Why don't you let the river do it?"

"Can the river saw trees into lumber?"

"Sure it can."

So they let some other saint go without a festival and used the money to buy a sawmill big enough to supply them with boards to make tables and chairs.

Then Stan said, "Why are you in the dark every night with just those little candles? Why don't you have electric lights?"

They said, "Electric lights? Why, only Oaxaca City, the capital, has electric lights! How can we have electric lights? We cannot afford it."

Stan said, "Let the river do it."

They were convinced by now that the river could do things, so they let another saint go without a festival and bought a hydroelectric plant through the electrical commission.

Then the priest called them in. He said, "Do you know that that foreigner is a heretic? He has not attended any of our church services since he has been here. He has not come to mass a single time. Get him out of here!"

The Indians said, "Father, he may be a heretic, but he is the only one who knows how to fix our machinery. He stays!"

Yes, SERVICE! Service in the name of Jesus Christ will open doors. We serve through literacy, working through the government. We serve through linguistics, loaning teachers to universities and to institutes which want to offer linguistic courses. We serve through medicine insofar as linguists can.

God really uses service.

Plenty of Pure Water
for San Pedro Soteapan

John Lind

When the town officials of San Pedro Soteapan became aware of a gravity system which the village of Ocotal Chico had built to bring clean spring water into that community, they requested that the SIL team which helped Ocotal Chico with technology go also to Soteapan to see what might be feasible there.

A spring was located less than two kilometers from the storage tank, with enough elevation for the water to flow by gravity from the spring to the storage tank.

The town decided to develop the spring and utilize this water source. They collected the necessary funds, bought the pipe, and installed the line with their own labor. No outside funds were used. The SIL team provided some technical assistance and the encouragement needed to help these men believe that they themselves could accomplish a task they had never tried before. Although they had practically no experience or training for such a project, their desire to have good water and their native skill and intelligence enabled them to build the system successfully.

As the town grew to about twenty-one hundred and the demand on the water system also increased, the town officials again asked the SIL team to help them evaluate the problem. A larger spring some distance away was located. The amount of water that could easily be utilized was in excess of five liters per second.

There were considerable obstacles, however. This much water would demand a three-inch pipeline. The fact that the spring came out of a cliff would require the first two hundred meters of pipe to be fastened to the cliff and/or supported by concrete pillars. Since the gravity drop in those first two hundred meters was only about half a meter, a four-inch line, at least, would be needed for that section. Because of exposure to the weather, the line would have to be galvanized steel, which could be very expensive. Two very difficult cliffside areas had to be traversed and the main fork of the river crossed. In addition, there were numerous other problems to solve in order to put in this line.

Having had the experience of the previous project several years before, in a 1982 community meeting the town decided, with typical Popoluca pluck and daring, to build the line and get the water they needed. Every man agreed to provide not only his share of the labor but also an appropriate part of the one and one-half pesos per person required to buy the material. The outgoing municipal president proceeded to buy three thousand meters of three-inch plastic pipe with town money. The new president bought twenty-five lengths of three-inch galvanized steel pipe and thirty lengths of four-inch galvanized pipe.

The terrain is very steep, rocky, and covered with large trees and brush. The men cleared the ground and then decided where the line could be put. An SIL team provided some suggestions, as needed, but the people themselves, especially those chosen by the community to head up the project, worked through the problems and found solutions. The man in charge of the water system, Ciriaco Cruz, explained his ideas for a swinging cable bridge and for using discarded train rails for support.

The main job of connecting the pipe, constructing the bridge, and building the spring tank was accomplished in a little over a week. On the first workday the men from Soteapan began to show up with boards, tools, and cement; they also helped carry pipe. On the third day Victor Pascual, municipal president, and his family provided a pleasant break. They brought a feast for all to enjoy as they sat on the hillside watching water run out of their new pipe!

The most clever piece of engineering of the entire project was the temporary bridge built to swing the pipe across the river. Using only machetes and material they found in the brush, the men built a platform.

They used trees with forks and placed the lower ends in spaces between the rocks. They used vines to tie the braces and posts, the crosspieces, and the floor poles. While they were gathering materials, others were carrying pipe and rails, about one hundred fifty men at a time. "Just like ants, swarming all over," they described themselves.

In addition, many hundreds of man-days were invested in clearing the jungle and digging the ditches beforehand. Everyone did his share of the work and learned much, both in actual skills and also in realizing what can be accomplished when people work together on a difficult job.

Another payoff from this project was an improvement in relations between Soteapan and one of its agencies, Ocotal Chico. The spring is inside the *ejido* of Ocotal Chico; a few people of that town had some objections to letting the larger town have "their" water. Then the leaders of the two places got together and worked out an agreement covering not only the water but also matters concerning grazing land for mules and horses, areas for cutting firewood, and materials for building houses. People in both towns were very pleased with the solutions.

The water is flowing into town and the people are happy with the amount of uncontaminated water the system provides. They recognize what this will mean for their health. The sense of satisfaction generated by the completion of this large project is beyond measure. The ingenious men of Soteapan faced and solved problem after problem. They were having fun. And SIL too was blessed.

High Corn Yield
for the Lealao Chinantec

James Rupp

"Your mothers could not nurse three or four babies at one time, could they?" the SIL member asked his Chinantec neighbors.

No, they agreed. A mother can hardly take care of one, and twins are definitely a problem.

"A corn field has the same problem," the linguist continued. "It cannot provide nourishment for four plants in one mound."

In 1968 Jim Rupp, his wife Nadine, and their two small daughters went to live among the Lealao Chinantec people of southern Mexico. Their primary job: to do linguistic studies of this complex tonal Indian language and produce a small quantity of literature, including translation of the New Testament. Their other goal: to see that the corn seed yields more abundantly on the meager farmland of this mountainous tropical forest area.

There is little, if any, flat land here. Most homes are tucked into the creases of these rugged mountains. Thin trails wind through the thick underbrush and across the scars of the charred slopes. For centuries these Chinantec have known only one farming method. Find a hillside you can stand on without tumbling down the steep incline. Cut down its trees and bushes. Set a torch to it. In the ashes, every three feet, plant four kernels of corn. As the plants grow during the summer, seven feet of rain may fall, washing the topsoil of the now exposed land down the hillside. When the corn will no longer grow in the remaining rocks, find another hillside.

Terracing could help the Chinantec, Rupp thought as he watched his neighbors trudge for hours past wasted land in search of new cornfields. When Chinantec food supplies dropped so low in the early 1970s that corn had to be flown in for two consecutive summers, he knew something had to be done soon.

Plants could thrive there; the thick forest gave evidence of that. But burned and stripped of its rich carpet of decaying matter, the land was little better than rocks for growing the daily food of these people. For every pound of corn he planted on a burned-off slope, the Chinantec farmer harvested only twenty pounds. With good soil, Rupp figured, a pound of corn could yield two or three hundred pounds.

The problem was more complicated than poor soil. Since most Chinantec cannot grow enough corn for themselves, they must also work to earn money for the corn they lack. But outside work does not leave a man enough time to develop a new farming method.

Terracing would come with a price—the wages that a Chinantec man would otherwise get working for someone else. In 1973, with funds from his own pocket, Rupp hired a corps of workers to terrace a quarter-acre parcel. The land was so steep that they could cut only three feet into the hillside with their shovels before hitting rock. Work was disappointingly slow. Then the men discovered that hoes worked more effectively than their shovels. Changing tools and using a homemade A-frame device for determining the contour of the terraces hastened the project. To the finished terraces they brought chicken fertilizer and compost.

Behind schedule, they planted a month later than anyone else. The Rupps asked themselves: Would the terraced corn grow bigger and healthier? Would the Chinantec believe that two seeds to a hole produce as well as four?

Harvest brought proof of the better way. Corn on the experimental field was ten feet tall. Eight pounds of seed yielded more than four hundred pounds, and it was at least five times larger.

"We're not glad the nonterraced, four-seeds-to-a-hole crop did poorly," say the Rupps, "but it afforded a beautiful contrast and showed the people what could be done."

Rupp offered to teach men of the village to terrace their fields, and the town president sent out thirty men one day for classes and twenty-two the next.

The following year others learned how to terrace and those who came consistently received, besides their wages, a share of the terraced land to serve them in years to come.

The third year they tried to use a rototiller a friend donated but there were too many mechanical problems. So they broke up the ground with hand tools and proceeded with planting. They applied commercial fertilizer, which was now available in sufficient quantity and cheaper than buying animal manure. The corn shot to ten feet high, and the stalks were lush. Those who thought nothing could be grown on the poor land reclaimed by Rupp were dumbfounded.

Because Jim had to be at a language workshop in central Mexico during the following year's harvest, the Chinantec brought in the crop by themselves. Rupp estimated each of the two one-acre plots yielded two tons—ten times the usual yield!

"Three days before we left the village, Lazaro Cruz came over with an ear-to-ear grin," Rupp recalls. "He said, 'I planted like you did (two instead of four kernels) and my ears of corn are whoppers!' His crop was on unterraced land and he wanted to begin to terrace."

Four more villagers recently bought hoes to terrace independently. "We saw them working in their fields as we flew out for the workshop," Rupp reports. "What a thrilling and satisfying sight!"

Chunks of time spent in farming projects have not hindered Rupp's primary work of linguistic studies. "Working alongside the men in the fields gave me plenty of opportunity to hear lots of Chinantec spoken," he says.

The terracing and another community project, plastering the town hall, have shown the Chinantec that the Rupps are there to help them in every way possible—that they are interested in them as persons.

Service without a Smile
Robert Griffin

Have you ever done something that made you wish you could rewind the tape and re-record it? That happened to me the day I flew to the southern end of Mindanao to bring out two of our translators for a workshop.

The weather was foul. For two hours I dodged low clouds and rain, all the while anticipating the forthcoming landing. I knew it would be hairy. The girls lived at the upper end of a narrow cul-de-sac canyon. Once a pilot entered the canyon, he was committed to land—somewhere! On the approach, flying between the clutching mountains, I bounced all over the sky, fighting the winds, the airplane tossing like a chip on the ocean. That wasn't all. At the approach end of the airstrip stood a spirit tree, an immense barrier that could not be chopped down because "the spirits lived in it." On every landing I feared my left wing would slice through that tree! This day I wondered if the whole airplane might be impaled.

But I made it. Finally on the ground, I wiped my forehead, thanking the Lord for a safe landing. Then I turned the plane around and taxied back to where the pile of cargo waited to be loaded. First we had to weigh it. They had sixty pounds too much! On a good day I would have said, "Never mind. Let's go." In a short time we would have burned off that extra sixty pounds in fuel.

But on a bad-weather day with the wind blowing every which way, and a short airstrip, I was not about to take off with that extra weight. Now the killer—do you know what made up that extra sixty pounds? A bucket of rice, and buried in that rice were cans of sardines. I said, "Look, let's leave it here. The sardines will keep. Give the rice to the people. I will buy you a hundred pounds of rice and a carton of sardines when we get to Nasuli."

No way. They had planned to take that rice! And those sardines! It was not negotiable! I was already nervous from the landing and I was nervous about the takeoff. Now I had to deal with two obstinate girls! It was not very pleasant; I argued heatedly. Finally there was nothing to do but give in. The only option was to make two trips with partial loads to another airstrip about fifteen minutes away. That meant an extra thirty minutes and another hairy landing. It also made me tight on fuel. I was distraught and angry at what I considered nonsense. But is this the way servants act? I knew better, but my anger and frustration were carrying the day.

Later, after we reached Nasuli, the Lord started to work on me. I had to go to those ladies and ask, "Will you please forgive me? I was not very nice." That promoted an apology on their part. All turned out well, but we learn some things the hard way, don't we?

For me it was another lesson on how to be a servant—this time within the "family."

B.

Show deference to religious organizations.

Airstrip in the Swamp

Jack and Flora Loshbough

"A health center? An airstrip? You say we could have those? If you build them, we will be happy to let you spend time in our villages talking about your God." Chief Mombenga was giving Jack Loshbough of Evangelical Free Church Mission permission to visit the eighteen villages of the Ngiri River swamp area in the province of Ubangi in northwestern Zaire.

It was 1983. Jack and some new Zairian Christians from the Limpoko church had taken a seven-hour trip down the Ngiri River to Bomole in a dugout canoe. Here the chief of the eighteen "swamp area" villages resides. Jack found him to be amiable and happy that this construction could happen in his jurisdiction; it would be not only a great benefit to his people but also a prestigious sign of progress! In fact, Chief Mombenga said that he would provide workers to build the airstrip if Jack would supervise the project.

The only feasible spot for an airstrip was an area in the swamp where a three-foot-wide path had once been built for a motorbike to travel on. Jack and the chief divided the proposed airstrip area into twelve sections, assigned according to village size. The chief contacted each village leader to send workers.

The motorbike path had long since grown up with trees and shrubs; a difficult clearing job was the first step in building the airstrip. Then the workers dug out chunks of dirt from the swamp—with shovels only—and passed one chunk at a time down the line of men. The last man placed it and packed it down. In this way the airstrip was built up five to six feet so that it would not flood during rainy seasons, eighteen hundred feet long and thirty feet wide. It took three and a half years to complete because it could be worked on only in the dry season, about five months out of the year.

In this entire Ubangi area, the size of Illinois and Indiana combined, there is only one mile of paved road. Limpoko is the last village reachable by road—and that a very rough one—and never in the rainy season, because logs always wash away. From there on down to the Lua and Zaire Rivers the only access to villages is by boat. When the airstrip was finished, a health center was built at Limpoko and staffed with two registered nurses. The airstrip also provides better access to other parts of the Ubangi province, such as Tandala, where a mission hospital is located, and Gemena, the main city of the province.

Who uses the airstrip? All the people of the area, indigenous and expatriates. For example, MAF flies in to take sick persons to the hospital—an eight-hour journey by road whittled to nineteen minutes by plane. A number of SIL teams, such as Harold and Virginia Smith in Gemena, are located in the Ubangi province. Several European staff members of a nearby Catholic hospital and their African patients find the airstrip valuable. It is available to all.

Much good has resulted from this project. Jack and his African Christian friends were able to spend time in all villages although sometimes with difficulty. Always careful to seek permission from local authorities, they occasionally found some who were not as cooperative as the area chief had been. One unreached-people village chief, a Catholic, forbade them to stay. However, villagers who had been listening to this hour-long conversation objected to their chief's decision. They wanted to hear what these outsiders had to say! The chief finally changed his mind and let the visitors stay.

Another result of the airstrip project was to illustrate the great good which can come from the cooperation of organizations with the same God- and people-serving goal. The first SIL team to settle in the area, Elaine Thomas and Margaret Hill, both from England, located in Tandala. There the Free Church Mission, happy to have SIL there to translate into Ngbaka, made their housing and center facilities available to the newcomers. Later Elaine and Margaret moved to Gemena, where the mission even built a house for them to use. Such kindness assisted them in their translation of the entire Bible into Ngbaka. Several other SIL teams, both support and translators, work in the province of Ubangi on seven languages.

No doubt the Lord is smiling to see His people, regardless of the umbrellas under which they labor, cooperate with love and singleness of purpose.

Happy Pappy

Merrill Piper

I was a *comecuras*—"priest eater," as the Mexicans say. When Larry Montgomery asked me to deliver a courtesy package to Padre Alegre at his Atalaya Catholic station in the Peruvian jungle, en route to my own destination, I exploded. "I did not come here to fly for the Catholics," I expostulated. "No way am I going to become an errand boy for them!"

I was a new kid on the block. Nothing wrong with my pilot licenses. I had become acclimated to the Amazon jungle's humid heat. I had even been checked out on the long Ucayali River route to one of our most remote Indian village posts. But I was not reconciled to doing anything for the Roman Catholic priest whose station lay halfway between our Yarinacocha center and the pin-point clearing where two of our linguists lived with the Indians.

"Merrill," sighed Larry, "if you refuse to do it, you have to talk to the old man upstairs."

Steaming, I headed for Townsend's place and marched in the front door without even knocking. Uncle Cam was there. He offered me a chair. I landed heavily into it and launched into my righteous complaint that I had not come to Peru to fly gear for Catholics! He listened patiently. When I ran out of breath he bade me continue. But I had sputtered to a stop.

Then it was his turn. Carefully he spelled out to me that God wanted us to minister to all inhabitants of the jungle and that they would not care how much we know until they know how much we care.

Unconvinced, I left and took off. Atalaya was a long way from Yarinacocha, but the distance did not cool my ire. I was not even amused by the private nickname our people had coined for referring to the Spanish priest among ourselves—Happy Pappy. All were careful to prevent the reverend father from hearing the irreverent title.

Refueling is the first order of the day for every pilot after landing. I was in the midst of that operation, sweating profusely as I climbed up and down the steep bank carrying five-gallon cans of gas to pour into the tank, when a stocky, bearded individual arrived at the river's edge and stuck out his hand, flashing at the same time a great grin. "Hi!" he exclaimed in his limited English. "Me Happy Pappy."

Disconcerted by the revelation that our private nickname had been discovered, I managed a weak smile and greeted him in my equally limited Spanish. I was amazed to discover the reason for his waiting so long to greet me—he had been squeezing fresh orange juice for me, bringing a cooling, delicious drink! Communication was sufficient for me to understand that he was now inviting me to overnight with him on my way back to Yarinacocha later that day. He had the only running water, indoor toilet, shower, and radio in the town and was graciously offering me the use of all his facilities. As I took off I had no intention, however, of accepting his hospitality because I believed I could fly far enough on my return to reach a Protestant mission station.

I was longer than anticipated at the Indian village where our SIL team lived; I could not return to the SIL center that night. As I approached Atalaya for additional fuel, I had a decision to make. Should I spend the night in Atalaya visiting Happy Pappy, or should I fly ten minutes more and stay with Protestant friends? In a grouchy mood, I landed at Atalaya for additional fuel. My first impulse was to refuel, take off, and visit my friends; yet I felt strangely compelled to spend the night in Atalaya.

Happy Pappy again came to the airplane bringing me a glass of fresh orange juice, again extending his invitation to spend the evening there. I accepted the invitation and, after securing the airplane for the night, went to his home. He thoughtfully provided a guard for the plane, to watch it for me in case the water rose or fell.

After we had eaten and were sitting on the veranda of his house, he pointed to his radio and suggested that I turn it on. Since it was very unusual for a Protestant to visit a Catholic priest at that remote jungle post, most of the several hundred inhabitants of the town were standing around the house listening with curiosity to our conversation. At this point it dawned on me why the Lord wanted me to spend the night in Atalaya. Hesitantly, I turned the radio on and tuned in station HCJB. With apprehension I glanced at Happy Pappy; he was sitting in his rocking chair, grinning from ear to ear, apparently enjoying the prospect of listening to the program. I turned the volume up as loud as it would go so the audience in the yard could hear as well. The program was in Spanish and included beautiful gospel music as well as a good sermon.

What a spectacle! An audience of several hundred Catholic nationals was listening to the gospel in excellent Spanish over the only radio in the village, which happened to be owned by a Catholic priest. Silently I thanked God for this opportunity to receive His love through this man; I had almost passed it up!

Happy Pappy invited me to come again, and I did many times. Every time we all listened to radio station HCJB!

A Case of Mistaken Identity

Richard Pittman

When we first went to the Philippines, the Roman Catholics had an eloquent lay spokesman fluent in both English and Tagalog, a professor in the leading Catholic university.

Whenever there was a "holy war" to be fought, this man was out front, writing brilliant letters and articles promoting the Roman

Catholic cause. By a fascinating "error," because of the similarity between his name and the name of another leading language expert, we started sending linguistic articles to the professor. By the time I discovered the mistake, the professor considered himself a friend because of the mailings. When we asked for office space, we were given space in his office in the Department of Education. Several of us had tremendous witnessing privileges with him as a result. By the time he was dying of cancer, many years later, he was delighted to have us come to his home, read the Bible to him, and pray with him. I have no doubt that we will see him in heaven.

When Billy Graham and other evangelists hold meetings in Manila, they frequently find themselves very well received in Catholic circles. Thousands of Catholics attend their meetings, often with the blessing of the Catholic officials. Some will say we should have been denouncing those officials in the press and from platforms. God has told us that remonstrance with them should be personal and private. I did just that with the professor, quoting many Scripture warnings and commands against idolatry. He listened patiently and quietly to my long exhortation. I personally am convinced that it bore fruit in his life and no doubt in the lives of others through him. His friendliness certainly mellowed my abrasiveness.

Several years later, Christian friends of ours in New Jersey were being put through the wringer by neighbors whose teenage boy tormented the children of our friends. They asked me if it was all right to call the police. "No," I said. "Perform acts of friendly neighborliness to the parents of the obnoxious boy and to the boy himself."

They said, "We have tried, but the parents are as bad as the boy. They indignantly reject all our overtures."

"Keep trying," I said. "Paul says that love never fails."

Perhaps a year later there was a sudden change. Our friends gave the offending boy a set of *Narnia* books. They told him they loved him. The hatchet was buried between the two families, and genuine peace, based not on police action but on New Testament procedures, was established. You can hardly imagine a happier family than the one who tried the love route against their oppressors and found, finally, that it worked.

Tim and Barbara Friberg were in Phnom Penh almost up to the time that the government there was taken over by the Khmer Rouge. Refugees were flooding into the capital, the number of wounded was astronomical, and even herculean efforts for feeding the countless thousands seemed futile. Tim wrote, "We are often overwhelmed by a feeling of hopelessness and helplessness. It seems that there is nothing we can do. But we find that there *are* things we can do to minister to these people when we tackle them one at a time."

It is an extremely significant statement. Blasts in the media, demonstrations, protests, explosions of anger and indignation are not God's way. God gives each of us just one opportunity of ministry at a time: one cup of cold water for one thirsty child, one bandage for one wound, one half-hour to visit one dying friend. It is no use throwing our one little lunch away with a sarcastic "What good is this when five thousand are hungry?"

High Praise

Translation of a reply to the Townsends' 1980 New Year's letter from a friend who was at one time alleged to be very antireligious.

My dear and admired Friend,

It was not possible for me to have the pleasure of writing you before this because I was in Puebla being treated for my broken health. I am now writing to send my affectionate greetings and to thank you for sending the quotation from my unforgettable chief and friend, General Lazaro Cardenas del Rio, who knew so well how to inject courage and enthusiasm into the magnificent cultural work which you and your wife Elaine carried on for several years on behalf of the Indian communities in Mexico.

I read with growing emotion the various aspects of the work being done by the Summer Institute of Linguistics, not only in Mexico but also in Peru, Colombia, and other nations. The labor which you, Elaine, your daughter Amalia, and your greathearted companions are doing is deeply moving. In all of your praiseworthy efforts there stands out in bold relief the profound human sentiment which animates you and the sacrifice which you make without recognizing distinctions of race, frontiers, castes, or political creeds. From whatever point of view a person takes, your contribution deserves high praise!

May the year 1980 be fruitful and filled with delightful and prosperous victory. And may you continue to enjoy the understanding and cooperation which you deserve, so as to be able to continue the heroic task to which your heart of brotherly love is so dedicated.

My profound respects to Elaine and a strong embrace for you from the affectionate servant who is addicted to your friendship.

May God Encourage You to Carry On

Translation of a speech by His Excellency Monsignor Javier Ariz, Bishop of Puerto Maldonaldo, speaking on behalf of His Eminence Cardinal Juan Landazuri Ricketts, at the dedication in 1979 of the New Testament newly translated into five Indian languages of Peru.

Minister Guabloche, Mr. Director of the Linguistic Institute, my dear Brothers and Friends in the Lord:

It is certainly a great honor for me to represent His Eminence the Cardinal, bringing a word of encouragement and blessing for this noble, beautiful, and fruitful effort which the Summer Institute of Linguistics has been carrying on for so many years. I do not believe that there is any more useful, important, and transcendental task than that of being a messenger of the Word of God. I believe sincerely that one of the most hopeful and encouraging signs of our time is the spread of the Word of God, the multiplication of portions of the Old and New Testaments in every language, an effort being jointly done by many thousands of people who consider it the most important mission of their lives to consecrate all their efforts to the spread of the Word of God.

It is important to recognize at this point that venerable patriarch of the spread of the Word of God, Dr. William Cameron Townsend. What importance he attached to the Word of God—the Bible! How respectfully he approached it! It is impossible to visit him without finding the conversation turned before long to some commentary on passages of the Word of God. I remember his saying to me one day, "Did you know Father Alberto Colunga?"

"Of course! He was my professor."

"What was he like?"

"He was a simple and humble man who moved everyone by his friendliness in spite of being such a highly qualified man."

"Well, though I am not on personal terms with him, I have a very great love for him because, of all the versions which I read and translate, he moves me most profoundly because he has a very personal feel for the things of God. He must be a very great soul. I wish that God would give me in my lifetime the privilege of traveling some day to Salamanca to have an intimate conversation with Padre Colunga."

This anecdote reveals how this man felt and still feels and how his heart is moved by the language of the Word of God. And I believe that today, in the face of so many events which stir the world, in the face of this tremendous earthquake in which it is not clear what will sink and what will float, when discouragement so often overwhelms us, we have never had more effective means to unite us all.

How can we do otherwise than bless with all our heart this herculean effort of the Summer Institute of Linguistics? How can we do other than bless it with great love and give always a welcome, when their principal mission is this: Bring the Word of God and make it accessible to all men whatever their condition, their situation, or their way of life. God grant that there may awaken in us in this beautiful and significant act the determination to consecrate ourselves wholly as messengers of the Word of God, interpreters of the Word of God. We are sometimes very weak, very diluted, not very generous when it comes to sharing responsibilities. We are afraid to soil ourselves by becoming involved. We are afraid we might deteriorate. We prefer to go it alone. We do not trust others. "What will happen to this if I leave it, if I go away?"

God is not like that. God has put His best gifts in our hands. How could He be unaware of our fear that we might soil ourselves or deteriorate? How could He not know that we might manipulate everything, and all values of this world, in our favor, to our advantage, with a possibly egotistical motive? Nevertheless, how generously and how lovingly He delivers to each one of us His mysteries, His doctrine, His message, His Word! That presence of His lives among men and in us. We should be interpreters, messengers, apostles, ministers of the Word of God. The Word of God, the Holy Scriptures, is the soul of evangelism; it is the essential constituent heart of the prophetic ministry in which we are called to participate.

For that reason, Brethren of the Linguistic Institute, with all my heart, in the name of the Catholic Church, in the name of His Eminence the Cardinal Primate, in the name of the Apostolic Nuncio (who could not come because of an unavoidable diplomatic commitment), with all my heart I pass on this word of encouragement. May God bless your effort! May the Lord encourage and stimulate you to carry on, completing this work and this calling which, of all possible ministries, is the most beautiful, the most noble, and, I dare say, the only ultimately effective one in the world.

Attitude and Altitude

Cameron Townsend

Dear JAARS Pilots:

In looking over your reports, I find that most of you have been doing relatively little flying for Roman Catholic missionaries the past year. This is doubtless because they do not ask for it. But we need to *seek* ways of demonstrating our policy of giving service to all.

I understand that one of you was unhappy about flying Catholic missionaries into an area where they were going to start a brand new mission station. My thoughts took me back a few years to the time when we were planning to open up a new translator's outpost in Colombia and the local priest stopped us. We condemned his attitude; yet that is the attitude that one of you had.

Are we to help people start a new center for teachings that do not agree with ours? Well, whose example have we been instructed to follow? Our heavenly Father's. He causes His sun to shine and His rain to fall on the just *and* the unjust. Please seek opportunities to demonstrate His attitude. Remember that the only godly way to *overcome* evil is with good. (Romans 12:21) Never try to stop evil with evil. To refuse to fly people to where they have a right to go is to resort to an evil as well as an undemocratic means of warfare. It will bring defeat to us rather than to the other fellow.

I shiver at the thought of what such tactics would do to our own work. It certainly will not hurt the fellow whose teachings do not agree with ours. He has been able to get where he wanted to go for centuries without us and he will still be able to. It is to our advantage to take him, for thus we demonstrate the spirit of our Lord.

John Mishler, our superintendent of aviation in Peru, sent me the following from a Catholic missionary pilot recently:

"In regards to flying your two linguists to the Pavas area, the answer is yes. A copy of the 'Articles of Incorporation of Wings of Hope' also reads:

"...to provide without charge, remuneration or profit, transportation and communication facilities for missionaries, medical missionaries, teachers, and other religious, educational, and medical workers, without distinction as to race or religion...

"Thus I am given the opportunity to cooperate with your people...and, I hope, in the same excellent manner in which you have cooperated with me."

From the above you will see just one of the countless blessings that have come from our policy of following Christ's command to do unto others as we would have others do unto us.

The Wycliffe Way

Cameron Townsend

We were criticized by an outstanding Christian leader in the United States, a brilliant editor of a Christian publication, for taking monks and nuns in our planes. So I wrote to him and said, "Suppose you were driving along in the desert where there was no food or water and you came upon a broken-down bus. There sat the bus driver, who looked like a rounder, just waiting to get to town to get drunk. One passenger was a priest headed for the next town to give a lecture against Protestantism. The other passenger was a Gideon, anxious to get to town to speak at the First Presbyterian Church and give his testimony.

"Now, what are you to do? You have room for three men in your car. Will you pick up all three of them and get them to safety? Or will you take just the Gideon and tell the rounder, 'I am not going to help you get drunk so you just stay here. Of course you may die of lack of water, but that is better than getting drunk. You stay.' Or would you take the driver and the Gideon, but leave the priest and say to him, 'You plan to get to that town and give a lecture against Martin Luther and all his followers; since I am a Protestant, I will leave you here.' Or would you pick up all three of them, put the priest up beside you in the front seat, and put that fellow that's anxious to get drunk beside the Gideon in the back seat and drive to town?"

The editor answered that he would wait until God had put him in such a predicament and then he felt that God would lead him. I replied that God had put us in such a situation and God had led us. With the priest in the front seat beside me I was sure that his speech would be mellowed when he got to town. With the bus driver beside the Gideon I was pretty sure he would be saved and not get drunk.

With few exceptions, every person who flies in our planes must pay for his ride. We transport first of all our Bible translators, but we also fly their national friends, government officials, religious people, and visitors as we have time and space. Do you think our pilot can give a doctrinal examination before he takes on passengers? "Wait now; can you sign this doctrinal statement? Are you evangelical, or are you Catholic? Or don't you believe at all?" And after the examination has been written out should he say, "You can ride; you're an evangelical. You're Catholic; you can't. You're an unbeliever; I won't take you." A pilot cannot do that. A pilot has to serve, serve the one who needs him most, serve everybody regardless of their doctrine. Service to all, service in love, service in the name of Jesus Christ. That's the Wycliffe way.

C.

Love your enemies.

Jammed Frequency

Kenneth Gammon

Gene Scott worked with the Sharanahuas on the Purus River, close to Brazil. The only way to get up to his village was by float plane. Finally I was assigned to help him build an airstrip so that wheel planes could land in his village and he could get air service whether the rivers were up or down, low or high.

While I was there, radio contact with Yarinacocha was almost impossible; there was almost always interference on our frequency—not just people talking, but music and Morse code. We could not do anything about it. We prayed that it would go away, but it never did. Occasionally we could have a sked in the evening, but it was a serious problem.

After the airstrip was finished and we were ready for a wheel plane to come, we needed to get some fuel out to the village. We had several drums of fuel in the town of Esperanza, downriver from Scotty a whole day's travel by outboard-driven canoe. A couple of the Sharanahua men and I went down to pick up the fuel. We got there a little late and knew we would not be able to get back that day, so we decided we would spend the night.

One of the priests at the Catholic mission in Esperanza invited us to supper. During the supper hour, as it began to get dark, we discovered that he did not have any lights. He said his generator did not work any more. I told him that I was a mechanic and would be glad to fix the generator. He said, "No, no, don't fix it. It's OK."

I knew something was wrong, but I did not know exactly what it was. I prayed silently about it and felt that God would have me try to fix the generator. I sort of pushed my way in on the thing. A couple of the Indians showed where the generator was, and I went out with my flashlight. I saw the generator. In the middle of the room next to the generator was the priest's radio, tuned in to an FM station. He had a little wire from the antenna of his radio over to a telegraph key. He would tune in Peruvian music on his radio station and send it on our frequency, together with dots and dashes, thus jamming our frequency at the time that we were trying to talk to Yarina.

I went ahead, fixed his generator, and got it running real well for him. He was red-faced when I told him I had the generator fixed. I told him what the problem was and how to repair it if it ever broke down in the future.

The priest never jammed Scotty's radio again.

Thanks for the Zapper!
Mark Ortman

My wife and I have recently started a translation project in the Tibesti Mountains of northern Chad in the Sahara Desert. After two preliminary trips to the area, we made our formal move there in April 1994, thinking we already had a house to live in. However, the whole process of finalizing this rental agreement was fraught with innumerable difficulties and bad will to the point at which, when we finally did move in, our landlord would barely shake our hands or look us in the eye.

Several days later he was stung by an enormous scorpion and came to us in great pain, asking for some medicine. It was our first time to use the JAARS zapper in the Tibesti and the results, in front of several local men, were miraculous! In less than ten minutes the cut he had made to suck out the poison was causing him more pain than the scorpion sting itself.

This was a turning point in our relationship. Things gradually improved until, by the time we departed, he had developed almost a fatherly concern for us.

All this came about because, before we left the States in 1991, Wayne Teague had given us one of the snakebite kits he had made for JAARS. How grateful we are to JAARS for providing this tool to aid not only in the translation task but also in showing our concern for others!

I Have "Her" on Board

Fred McKennon

I have sat in meetings where Uncle Cam reminded us to love our "enemies," to be kind to them, and to serve them. God gave me a personal experience of this kind in March 1979.

Some three years earlier the bilingual school system in Peru was decentralized from the Ministry of Education, and administration was put in the hands of the *nucleos* (regional schools), which are right out where the bilingual teachers are. This was good in some areas but caused difficulties in others. In one place the local administrators even burned some of the books that were published for the bilingual school system. In one area, San Lorenzo on the lower Maranon, there was a former nun who was given authority to direct this program in the jungle. Some of the bilingual teachers were fired; others were harassed. We tend to consider such administrators our "enemies," but Leo Lance urged us to pray for this person rather than hate her.

One day in March I had a trip out to Barranca with supplies for Peruvian young people working alongside SIL. As I prepared to leave, the *comandante* asked if I would transport one of his teachers. I said, "Sure, I'm going back empty, and I would be happy to take your teacher." I put her and her baggage into the plane.

As I was making the last check, making sure everything was ready for takeoff, a missionary met me at the far wing. He said, "Do you know whom you have on board?"

I said, "No, I don't."

He said, "That's the one who has been giving all these problems to the bilingual school effort."

I did not know what to say—she was in the airplane and all ready to go. So I said, "Great. Let's go."

I took off and God impressed me that I should get in touch with the center. I did not know how to do that discreetly. Our aircraft frequency is routinely monitored, so I decided to try to get hold of Leo, who was our chief pilot and who was also flying. I tuned to VHF (Very High Frequency) and said, "I have X on board. What shall I do?"

He said, "Call the director." I changed to the right frequency and called Eugene Loos. All he said when he found out whom I had on board was "I'll see you at the airplane." I was going a little faster than anticipated—had a tailwind—so I slowed the airplane a bit, got the gear down, and made sure that Eugene would be there when I arrived.

Sure enough, when I landed he was there. I taxied up to the pad and shut down. By the time I got out he had already opened the door and introduced himself to the passenger. He took her bag, and they were standing beside the wing when I walked up. She turned to me and said, "How much do I owe you?"

I referred her to Eugene, who replied, "This is by courtesy of the Institute." Then he offered her a ride in a vehicle that was going into Pucallpa and put our center services at her orders—whatever she needed.

Because of the way she had been treating us and the bilingual school system, she felt embarrassed. She tried to take her bag out of Eugene's hand and head for the lake to hire transport. But Eugene kept the bag and went with her to the lake edge. The Lord saw to it that no commercial transport came, so they stood there making conversation. Leo went in and got a cool drink for her. The last I saw my passenger, she was going up the hill on the back of Eugene's motor scooter.

The next Sunday Eugene spoke in our morning service and told the rest of the story. He chauffeured her as his guest around the facilities on the center. When she finally started for Pucallpa in the vehicle that she had been offered by Eugene, she turned to him and said how overwhelmed she was at the kindness she had received on the flight and during her short time there.

Come for Tea

Cameron Townsend

It is a custom to tip your hat to a man in Latin America, but one missionary in Peru would not tip his hat to a priest, nor say good day. Saying good day is wishing the priest prosperity, he believed, so he would not do it. One American priest, a Franciscan, said, "After all, we are fellow Americans. At least we could be friendly one to another, couldn't we?" Still the missionary felt that he was compromising if he showed any friendliness to the priest. That attitude does not win the battle. If you can play Ping-Pong with that priest, if you can invite him home for a meal, if you can do him some favor like transport him in your plane, by all means do so. It wets his gun powder and it may win his heart.

One of our couples had gone way back into the jungle of Ecuador on the Aguarico River, where there was a small ethnic group. They got a landing strip started so the plane could bring them in, take them out, and bring supplies. They were winning the confidence of the Indians, when a Spanish priest came and started a mission at the end of their landing strip. What were they going to do?

Mrs. Johnson said, "I know what to do. He will enjoy some good food."

Her husband went to the priest and said, "My wife would like you to come try some of her cooking."

He came once. Then he said, "Listen, we are enemies. I cannot come and eat at your table this way."

"Well, at least come and take tea with us in the afternoon."

"Okay, I will come and take tea with you."

He was a lonely man. The Indians could not talk his language. He wanted a little fellowship, but I suppose he had been ordered by his superior not to be friendly. After he had taken tea a few times, he began remembering that good food he had had.

Mary said, "Won't you come and have a dinner with us?"

"Okay, I'll come." He stuck it out for a year and a half; then he disappeared and the mission was closed down. The last we heard of him he had gone to some place in the Philippines. He was completely whipped by love.

For six years there were seemingly no results in that area. But now the work is going forward and many are turning to the Lord. A young Ecuadorian man has learned to be a teacher. The government pays his salary and he has a school there. Win your enemies by love, or, if you want to put it another way, whip your enemies by love. Lincoln said, "Annihilate your enemies by love." Make them friends. It is all the same thing. It is overcoming evil with good.

If You Meet Visitors, Mag-adjust*!

Andrew Gallman

Sherry and I were looking for a place to live with a group who needed Scriptures. Seymour offered to accompany me on a trip to seek a site. All seemed auspicious, including even the fabulous beauty of the remote valley we were headed for. I did not sense any cryptic message in the advice of a friend, "If you meet visitors, mag-adjust."

But the intent of the advice became painfully clear when, the day after our arrival at our destination, a heavily armed patrol of dissidents arrived too. They wanted to meet us, so Seymour invited them for supper.

Not even the presence of a comely armed young woman with the ten men allayed my apprehension. "She is my sweetheart," the leader explained. "We plan to get married soon."

There is something about a passel of rifles, pistols, and machine guns which makes the heart beat faster. At least, mine did. The artillery proved very persuasive when members of the patrol explained their "needs." I felt quite free, therefore, to share my soup, shirts, and food supplies as various ones appropriated them.

Not so my camera. "I need that myself," I remonstrated. "And although I am happy to help you as a fellow human being in need, to give you my camera would be to help your cause rather than to help you." I reached over and took the camera back. The young man who had taken it looked astonished but did not resist.

Seymour, no doubt as deeply concerned as I, never lost his cool. Chatting in a friendly, hospitable way, he described our work and related to the visitors as any nonbelligerent should.

Time came when we should part. But would they let us? They were armed and we were not. The site was far, far from the nearest police or army post. They could easily have held us for ransom or, at the very least, taken the rest of our belongings from us.

"Friend," said Seymour to the leader of the patrol, "since you and your lady friend are planning to be married, I would like to give you a wedding present. Here," he said, taking the wristwatch off his wrist and handing it to the bandit. "Please keep this as a souvenir of our encounter."

"You don't need to do that!" exclaimed the other, but he accepted the gift. Tension, which had been building as everyone wondered how (and if) we would part, drained away. Smiles broke out on previously frowning faces. We shook hands all around. The dissidents went their way and we went ours. The village sighed with relief.

*mag—a prefix used in one country to make a verb have an un-equivocal sense of deliberate, intentional, intelligent action.

Shall We Call Down Fire from Heaven?

Richard Pittman

I have mostly avoided Jeremiah. His book seems at times to be a counsel of despair. It seems especially unhelpful for us "fighting" types who would like to roll up our sleeves and wade into the fray.

The problem is that Jeremiah, like the other sixty-five books of the Bible, is inspired and has something to say to us from the Lord.

American Christians in the early 1980s had the enviable privilege of being mostly uninvolved in shooting wars. There is a perception, however, of evil and danger in many places, against which good people should speak out. Not the least of those we should castigate, some believe, are the undesirable and oppressive governments of other countries.

The problem is that denunciation of governments other than our own has mischievous consequences:

1. It can exacerbate relations between two countries, damaging efforts at peace and heightening the tensions which lead to war.

2. It can close doors to the gospel which might otherwise be open.

3. Ears which might be open to appeals for reconciliation can be stoppered by a perception of raucous malevolence given by those making denunciations.

4. It not infrequently happens that stone throwers live in glass houses.

5. Public denunciations can destroy private efforts at reform which may have great promise because they help real or alleged malefactors to save face.

6. RAO (Responsibility Assumption Overload) damage done to the one denouncing can be very great. Those suffering most may be innocent, uninvolved people neglected by the RAO or hurt by a backlash.

7. If the motive of a denunciation is revenge, a specific violation of a Scriptural prohibition can result: "Dearly beloved, avenge not yourselves, for it is written, 'Vengeance is mine, I will repay,' saith the Lord."

The three disciples closest to Jesus must have started out, all of them, as firebrands. Peter cut off Malchus' ear. James and John wanted to call down fire on an inhospitable village of Samaria. But Jesus rebuked them all.

Lord, is there any hope that we can learn?

I Am a Neighbor of Yours

Excerpts from a talk by Richard Pittman at a ceremony dedicating the "Friendship of Minnesota-Henry Coleman Crowell Memorial" airplane for service in the Philippines.

Shortly after World War II, at a time when the Huks were strong in Central Luzon, Philippines, a longtime friend of SIL, Mr. Zosimo Montemayor, was president of Central Luzon Agricultural College. But the Huks were giving him a hard time because they were illegally logging in a forest which belonged to the college.

President Montemayor decided to investigate. Alone and unarmed, he walked to the area where the Huks lived. Arriving there, he found a big feast in progress. Without introducing himself, he sat down at one of the tables and joined in the feasting. Suddenly a leader spotted him. "Hey!" he blurted. "Who are you?"

"I am a Filipino," replied Monty, unperturbed.

"What are you doing here?" his challenger demanded.

"I am helping you celebrate," was the unruffled reply, as he continued to eat.

"Who are you?" the inquisitor probed.

"I am Zosimo Montemayor. I am a neighbor of yours."

By the time the truth was fully out, the temper of the questioner had cooled and a friendly dialogue had begun. Before it ended, Monty had worked out an arrangement whereby the Huks would be allowed to continue meeting their logging needs but would contribute to the Agricultural College a certain proportion of the logs which they cut.

God has given to the Filipinos a genius for reconciliation. Not only was Zosimo Montemayor remarkable in that respect, but also the late President Magsaysay, and a host of others. It is a great privilege to be associated with such a nation.

One reason it means so much to us is that God has also committed to us a ministry of reconciliation. Years ago I was riding in an airplane from New Guinea to Manila. Having with me a collection of Bible readings which began with a story about Abraham, I offered it to the man sitting next to me to read. He looked at the title of the first story, looked at me, and said, "I am a son of Abraham." Then he launched into a long, bitter recital of the sufferings which he and his Jewish people had received from Christians. Finally he said, "I know that some Jews bring suffering on themselves because they are bad. But not all of us are bad."

That was my chance. I said, "Some people who profess to be Christians are also bad. But not all Christians are bad! In fact," I continued, "a true Christian cannot be anti-Semitic because he is depending on a Jew, Jesus Christ, to save him."

Then I pulled a Bible out of my briefcase and turned to Ephesians 2. Explaining that Paul, a Jew, was writing to Gentiles, I read, "You Gentile believers were once aliens from the commonwealth of Israel and strangers to the covenant of promise, having no hope and being without God in the world. But now in Christ Jesus, you who once were far off have been brought near by the blood of Christ. For He is our peace. He has made us both one. He has broken down the dividing wall of hostility between us...that He might create in Himself one new man in place of two...and might reconcile us both to God in one body through the cross, thereby bringing the hostility to an end."

"I have never heard those things before!" exclaimed my new friend. And as he left me in Manila he said, "I will not forget!"

God has given to the Philippines, with its remarkable history and location, not only a responsibility of reconciliation between East and West, Old and New, Asian and American, but also a leading role of mediation between Christian and Moslem, monotheists and polytheists, the cultural majority and many cultural minorities. The Summer Institute of Linguistics is highly honored to be permitted to serve the Philippines with linguistics, literacy, Bible translation, and air transportation. And we are deeply conscious of the fact that this is possible only because of the prayerful help of such friends as you in Minnesota and the "extended family" of the late Henry C. Crowell.

Jericho Walls

Cameron Townsend

So often I think of the children of Israel marching around those tremendous walls of Jericho. Day after day, day after day until the seventh day. And how many times did they have to go around on the seventh day? Seven times. Seven and six—thirteen times. The whole group of—a million, was it? They had to march around those walls. What if they had not done it? What if they had said, "We have gone around ten times now and nothing has tumbled; there is no sign of the walls falling"? Joshua had instructions which said thirteen times around; then the walls tumbled. Wycliffe, from the early days, has found that what makes the walls of Jericho fall down is service. Serving this way, serving that way, finding ways of service. Cooperation, working hand in hand, letting the other fellow have the glory, the credit.

In one country we served the priest at the mouth of the Putumayo River. We took the priest some goodies that Elaine fixed. We showed him some attention. Whenever we went there we visited with him. We gave him a book of C.H. Spurgeon's sermons translated into Spanish. We understood that he was using them Sunday after Sunday as long as they lasted. It paid off. The bishops decided to fight us to get rid of us. They brought him into the capital—got him drunk—and in that condition had him sign a statement against us. But as soon as he was sober he was again favoring us, showing us kindness and courtesies.

The bishops prohibited their priests from riding in our airplanes. The president of the country wanted a divorce from his wife of forty years, and we were told that one condition on which the pope would give him the divorce was that he fight us. So he named the Minister of War to lead the attack on us.

A bishop was trying to get a priest and about a dozen brothers to go out on the Purus River and there was no way of getting them there. The government DC-3 flew out with one of the priests on board and almost had a wreck. The air force said that they would not fly them. We had a Catalina that Mexico had given us in recognition of the service we had performed for the Indians in Mexico. That of course could land on the river—so we offered the services of the plane, but the bishop would not accept it.

Months went by and finally he gave in. "All right," he said, "the missioners will travel on your Catalina." But he would not let a newspaperman go along. So we took a picture with the priests and nuns beside our Catalina airplane with our pilots.

As soon as the picture was developed I took it to the Minister of War. He looked at it and said, "The priests say that Townsend is out there fighting them! Here he is transporting them in planes." He showed it to a group of generals gathered at a committee meeting and from then on we had no opposition from them or from the Minister of War.

Then the four archbishops published a statement signed by each stating that the government must get rid of the Summer Institute of Linguistics. The president was out of the country, so for a few days things looked bad. When he got back, he called in one of the bishops and said, "I am Roman Catholic but I want the Summer Institute of Linguistics to continue here and I want you to keep your mouth shut." Word went out that the president was for us. He protected us.

An attack and a letter

One time in the early days the main newspaper in the capital published an attack on us, so the Lord guided me to write a letter explaining what we were doing and why we were doing it. I took it to the newspaper publisher. He said, "The priests are against you and we are against you." Then he read the letter and decided to publish it all.

I stopped on the street the next day and talked to one of the outstanding educators of Peru. He said, "Townsend, I read your letter. I agree with you one hundred percent. I am right behind you." That was the way the government responded when they knew the facts. They took care of us.

Years later we came on a newspaper clipping saying we would have to leave and turn over all our properties to the government. Not long afterwards God raised up General Guabloche. He went to bat for us as Minister of Education. He gave us a contract extension.

Yes, those valleys of the shadow of death have to be traversed. God gives the victory, but we must remember to keep up the march around the walls of Jericho. It may not seem to accomplish anything, but the walls will tumble. We worked with the government to establish a system of bilingual education for Indians. The day came when classes were given in twenty Indian languages of the jungle. We did it in the name of the government, under the umbrella of the government.

A well-to-do friend had invited us to her home and we entertained the Minister of Education there. A day or two later the minister called the educators, the head men of the ministry, together. He said, "Here is what I decided we are going to do. We are going to train bilingual Indian teachers and establish schools among their people. The Summer Institute of Linguistics is going to help us. They will provide linguists; they will go back into the villages and select gifted Indians to come and take the course. Now, I want you to know that I did not agree to this program under the influence of liquor. At the table of the Summer Institute of Linguistics we were lucky to get lemonade!"

Yes, another circle around the wall of Jericho and the wall came tumbling down!